THE STEP BY STEP

KUPPET

AIR FRYER

COOKBOOK

EASY, QUICK AND DELICIOUS RECIPES

FOR BEGINNERS

ADOLPH FUNK

CONTENTS

INTRODUCTION

The Operation Principle of KUPPET Air Fryer

What's the secret to this appliance's magic? When you break it down, an air fryer is essentially a miniature convection oven that evenly circulates hot air around your food. Air fryers contain a fan that rapidly moves the heated air around, helping your food to crisp up without much additional oil. It also has the ability to reach very high temperatures (with some models getting up to 430F°) enhancing its ability to quickly cook foods. The device is ideal for anyone keeping a close eye on their fat consumption, as you only need a thin coat of oil on the food or on the cookware surface to prevent sticking and achieve a golden, crispy crunch. Not only does it fry, but the air fryer can also mimic other cooking functions such as baking, grilling and roasting.

Keep in mind that an air fryer is ideal for making foods in small quantities simply because the appliance does not have the physical capacity to hold a lot of food at one time. Most models can hold a from 3.5 quarts to 5.5 quarts in their fry baskets. The fry basket is the main accessory that comes with an air fryer, but some models can include other elements such as a baking pan or roasting rack. Being that the air fryer is similar to a convection oven (but way smaller), it can save you time (and electricity) over heating up your standard oven. It cooks food freakishly fast and the clean up fuss-free.

The Advantages of KUPPET Air Fryer

Air fryers have gained popularity in recent months due to the increased health awareness and more people taking deliberate action to ensure they live a healthy lifestyle. These air fryers have a lot of benefits to offer, some of which are highlighted below:

1. Cook Multiple Dishes

You can cook multiple dishes at once with an air fryer which would save you a lot of time. This is like having a skillet, a deep fryer, a toaster, and an oven together in one machine. There are also several healthy dishes you can make with it; for example, the air fryer salmon recipes. Salmon is known for its many health benefits and with an air fryer in place, you can worry less about ever having trouble cooking this fish. Other recipes you can try include the Crispy Air Fryer Baked Potatoes, Crispy Air Fryer Bacon, Air Fryer Mozzarella Sticks, Air Fryer Chocolate Chip Cookies, and Air Fryer Buttermilk Fried Chicken, among others.

2. It Helps Promote Weight Loss

Several studies have shown how fried foods can increase the risk of weight gain and obesity and other cardiovascular problems. In a study conducted in 2019 on mortality in women in the United States, it was found that "the frequent consumption of fried foods, especially fried chicken and fried fish/shellfish, was associated with a higher risk of all cause and cardiovascular mortality in women in the US".

However, you don't have to completely give up your favorite meals that require deep frying. A healthier option will be to use an air fryer for all fried meals, as it reduces your regular take of unhealthy oils, which promotes weight loss. Weight loss also reduces your risk of other health complications, including cardiovascular disease.

3. It is Safe to Use

One of the major troubles of deep frying is the risk of hot oil accidents or the consistent splashing of oil while frying. With air fryers, you can worry less about this, as there's no risk of spilling or splashing of oil. You also do not have to worry about your kids being around the kitchen. It has an auto shut feature that is activated once cooking is completed, so you don't have to worry about overheating or burnt food.

The safety standards of air fryers make them more suitable compared to the traditional deep frying method.

4. It Reduces the Risk of Toxic Acrylamide Formation

Acrylamide formation is mostly caused by high-temperature cooking such as frying, roasting, or baking. This compound is dangerous and increases the risk of various cancers, including endometrial, ovarian, pancreatic, breast, and esophageal cancers. You can however reduce this risk by using an air fryer.

The Preparations for Air-Frying Use

1. Prepare the Food You'll Be Cooking

Like in any other cooking methodology, the very first thing you should do is to prepare the food you'll be cooking. Most ingredients aren't always bite size and ready to cook, so you have to do the washing, peeling, and chopping in this step, mostly. If you're going to cook a ready-to-eat frozen product, all you'll really need to do is take it out of the freezer. Most air fryers will be able to cook it nicely straight out of the fridge, making them very convenient options for quick meals.

Those who like to make their fried dishes with batter, check with your air fryer's manufacturer whether they can work with such before doing anything. If you're going to use wet ingredients like meat and freshly washed veggies, make sure to pat them dry first as well. This way, your air fryer won't have to work extra to dry the food and get to use its capacity to actually cook your food efficiently.

You can also wrap your ingredients with aluminum foil if you want to make the most out of your cooking basket's space. This will let you cook two different dishes in one go without the need for any accessory.

2. Prepare Your KUPPET Air Fryer

Once your ingredients are prepped, the next step is to prepare your air fryer. If you're going to use accessories, grab them now. It's best to have them on hand so you can also clean them up if they need some rinsing.

You should also check if the air fryer is clean and dry before plugging it in and starting it up. Crusted old food can affect the taste and smell of your dish, so it's best to make sure that your air fryer is completely clean before using it.

3. Preheat Your KUPPET Air Fryer

While this is still a part of preparing your appliance for cooking, it's still worth a special mention because it's something a lot of people tend to forget.

To preheat, set the appliance to the highest heat level and leave it on for five minutes. That will do the trick to heat up your unit nicely in just a short amount of time.

4. Load the Ingredients into the KUPPET Air Fryer

Once the air fryer is already hot, it's ready to start cooking. Load the ingredients into its cooking basket. Make sure to use the right accessories if you intend to use them. Also, make sure to use them properly so you can make the most out of them.

5. Make Sure Not to Crowd the Cooking Basket

While loading your ingredients into the air fryer, another key trick how to use an air fryer is to avoid crowding the basket. Your ingredients will need all the space it can get so it can be exposed to hot air, while the hot air also needs room to move around.

Don't think that you'll get away with filling the basket to the brim as that will only lead to an undercooked mess.

6. Add a Bit of Oil to the Cooking Basket

The next thing you should do is to add some oil into your air fryer. While you can skip the oil entirely, it's still useful if you want to make sure that your ingredients won't stick together or to the basket while cooking. It will also give your dish the fried taste that only cooking with oil can give.

The Tips for Cleaning KUPPET Air Fryer

After your delicious meal is finished, it's time to clean your air fryer. We recommend cleaning your air fryer every time you use it, but the process of cleaning is not as daunting as you think.

➢ Unplug air fryer and take out the basket and the pan.

➢ Take a microfiber cloth and dampen it with hot water to clean the exterior of the appliance. Then, to clean the interior take a non-abrasive sponge and scrub the interior of the fryer.

➢ Next, clean the heating element by turning your air fryer upside-down and gently scrub it with a sponge.

➢ Most of the baskets and pans are dishwasher-safe, so load them into your dishwasher and let the dishwasher do the work. If you want to clean it yourself—hot water, dish soap, and a non-abrasive sponge will do the trick.

➢ If there's tough residue on your baskets and pans, soak them in hot water for about 10 minutes. Then scrub the residue away with a non-abrasive sponge.

➢ All that's left to do is to dry your appliance. We recommend to air dry the individual parts, but you can also take a cloth to dry the appliance. After it's all dry, put it back together and you'll be ready to tackle your next tasty air fryer recipe.

BEEF , PORK & LAMB RECIPES

California Burritos

Servings: 4 | Cooking Time: 17 Minutes

Ingredients:

- 1 pound sirloin steak, sliced thin
- 1 teaspoon dried oregano
- 1 teaspoon ground cumin
- ½ teaspoon garlic powder
- 16 tater tots
- ⅓ cup sour cream
- ½ lime, juiced
- 2 tablespoons hot sauce
- 1 large avocado, pitted
- 1 teaspoon salt, divided
- 4 large (8- to 10-inch) flour tortillas
- ½ cup shredded cheddar cheese or Monterey jack
- 2 tablespoons avocado oil

Directions:

1. Preheat the air fryer to 380°F.

2. Season the steak with oregano, cumin, and garlic powder. Place the steak on one side of the air fryer and the tater tots on the other side. (It's okay for them to touch, because the flavors will all come together in the burrito.) Cook for 8 minutes, toss, and cook an additional 4 to 6 minutes.

3. Meanwhile, in a small bowl, stir together the sour cream, lime juice, and hot sauce.

4. In another small bowl, mash together the avocado and season with ½ teaspoon of the salt, to taste.

5. To assemble the burrito, lay out the tortillas, equally divide the meat amongst the tortillas. Season the steak equally with the remaining ½ teaspoon salt. Then layer the mashed avocado and sour cream mixture on top. Top each tortilla with 4 tater tots and finish each with 2 tablespoons cheese. Roll up the sides and, while holding in the sides, roll up the burrito. Place the burritos in the air fryer basket and brush with avocado oil (working in batches as needed); cook for 3 minutes or until lightly golden on the outside.

Meat Loaves

Servings: 4

Cooking Time: 19 Minutes

Ingredients:

- Sauce
- ¼ cup white vinegar
- ¼ cup brown sugar
- 2 tablespoons Worcestershire sauce
- ½ cup ketchup
- Meat Loaves
- 1 pound very lean ground beef
- ⅔ cup dry bread (approx. 1 slice torn into small pieces)
- 1 egg
- ⅓ cup minced onion
- 1 teaspoon salt
- 2 tablespoons ketchup

Directions:

1. In a small saucepan, combine all sauce ingredients and bring to a boil. Remove from heat and stir to ensure that brown sugar dissolves completely.

2. In a large bowl, combine the beef, bread, egg, onion, salt, and ketchup. Mix well.

3. Divide meat mixture into 4 portions and shape each into a thick, round patty. Patties will be about 3 to 3½ inches in diameter, and all four should fit easily into the air fryer basket at once.

4. Cook at 360°F for 18 minutes, until meat is well done. Baste tops of mini loaves with a small amount of sauce, and cook 1 minute.

5. Serve hot with additional sauce on the side.

Kielbasa Chunks With Pineapple & Peppers

Servings: 2

Cooking Time: 10 Minutes

Ingredients:

- ¾ pound kielbasa sausage
- 1 cup bell pepper chunks (any color)
- 1 8-ounce can pineapple chunks in juice, drained
- 1 tablespoon barbeque seasoning
- 1 tablespoon soy sauce
- cooking spray

Directions:

1. Cut sausage into ½-inch slices.
2. In a medium bowl, toss all ingredients together.
3. Spray air fryer basket with nonstick cooking spray.
4. Pour sausage mixture into the basket.
5. Cook at 390°F for approximately 5minutes. Shake basket and cook an additional 5minutes.

Korean-style Lamb Shoulder Chops

Servings: 3

Cooking Time: 28 Minutes

Ingredients:

- ⅓ cup Regular or low-sodium soy sauce or gluten-free tamari sauce
- 1½ tablespoons Toasted sesame oil
- 1½ tablespoons Granulated white sugar
- 2 teaspoons Minced peeled fresh ginger
- 1 teaspoon Minced garlic
- ¼ teaspoon Red pepper flakes
- 3 6-ounce bone-in lamb shoulder chops, any excess fat trimmed
- ⅔ cup Tapioca flour
- Vegetable oil spray

Directions:

1. Put the soy or tamari sauce, sesame oil, sugar, ginger, garlic, and red pepper flakes in a large, heavy zip-closed plastic bag. Add the chops, seal, and rub the marinade evenly over them through the bag. Refrigerate for at least 2 hours or up to 6 hours, turning the bag at least once so the chops move around in the marinade.

2. Set the bag out on the counter as the air fryer heats. Preheat the air fryer to 375°F .

3. Pour the tapioca flour on a dinner plate or in a small pie plate. Remove a chop from the marinade and dredge it on both sides in the tapioca flour, coating it evenly and well. Coat both sides with vegetable oil spray, set it in the basket, and dredge and spray the remaining chop(s), setting them in the basket in a single layer with space between them. Discard the bag with the marinade.

4. Air-fry, turning once, for 25 minutes, or until the chops are well browned and tender when pierced with the point of a paring knife. If the machine is at 360°F, you may need to add up to 3 minutes to the cooking time.

5. Use kitchen tongs to transfer the chops to a wire rack. Cool for just a couple of minutes before serving.

Pork & Beef Egg Rolls

Servings: 8   Cooking Time: 8 Minutes

Ingredients:

- ¼ pound very lean ground beef
- ¼ pound lean ground pork
- 1 tablespoon soy sauce
- 1 teaspoon olive oil
- ½ cup grated carrots
- 2 green onions, chopped
- 2 cups grated Napa cabbage
- ¼ cup chopped water chestnuts

- ¼ teaspoon salt
- ¼ teaspoon garlic powder
- ¼ teaspoon black pepper
- 1 egg
- 1 tablespoon water
- 8 egg roll wraps
- oil for misting or cooking spray

Directions:

1. In a large skillet, brown beef and pork with soy sauce. Remove cooked meat from skillet, drain, and set aside.

2. Pour off any excess grease from skillet. Add olive oil, carrots, and onions. Sauté until barely tender, about 1 minute.

3. Stir in cabbage, cover, and cook for 1 minute or just until cabbage slightly wilts. Remove from heat.

4. In a large bowl, combine the cooked meats and vegetables, water chestnuts, salt, garlic powder, and pepper. Stir well. If needed, add more salt to taste.

5. Beat together egg and water in a small bowl.

6. Fill egg roll wrappers, using about ¼ cup of filling for each wrap. Roll up and brush all over with egg wash to seal. Spray very lightly with olive oil or cooking spray.

7. Place 4 egg rolls in air fryer basket and cook at 390°F for 4minutes. Turn over and cook 4 more minutes, until golden brown and crispy.

8. Repeat to cook remaining egg rolls.

Perfect Strip Steaks

Servings: 2

Cooking Time: 17 Minutes

Ingredients:

- ➢ 1½ tablespoons Olive oil
- ➢ 1½ tablespoons Minced garlic
- ➢ 2 teaspoons Ground black pepper
- ➢ 1 teaspoon Table salt
- ➢ 2 ¾-pound boneless beef strip steak(s)

Directions:

1. Preheat the air fryer to 375°F (or 380°F or 390°F, if one of these is the closest setting).

2. Mix the oil, garlic, pepper, and salt in a small bowl, then smear this mixture over both sides of the steak(s).

3. When the machine is at temperature, put the steak(s) in the basket with as much air space as possible between them for the larger batch. They should not overlap or even touch. That said, even just a ¼-inch between them will work. Air-fry for 12 minutes, turning once, until an instant-read meat thermometer inserted into the thickest part of a steak registers 127°F for rare (not USDA-approved). Or air-fry for 15 minutes, turning once, until an instant-read meat thermometer registers 145°F for medium (USDA-approved). If the machine is at 390°F, the steaks may cook 2 minutes more quickly than the stated timing.

4. Use kitchen tongs to transfer the steak(s) to a wire rack. Cool for 5 minutes before serving.

Lamb Meatballs With Quick Tomato Sauce

Servings: 4   Cooking Time: 8 Minutes

Ingredients:

- ½ small onion, finely diced
- 1 clove garlic, minced
- 1 pound ground lamb
- 2 tablespoons fresh parsley, finely chopped (plus more for garnish)
- 2 teaspoons fresh oregano, finely chopped
- 2 tablespoons milk
- 1 egg yolk
- salt and freshly ground black pepper
- ½ cup crumbled feta cheese, for garnish
- Tomato Sauce:
- 2 tablespoons butter
- 1 clove garlic, smashed
- pinch crushed red pepper flakes
- ¼ teaspoon ground cinnamon
- 1 (28-ounce) can crushed tomatoes
- salt, to taste

Directions:

1. Combine all ingredients for the meatballs in a large bowl and mix just until everything is combined. Shape the mixture into 1½-inch balls or shape the meat between two spoons to make quenelles (little three-sided footballs).

2. Preheat the air fryer to 400°F.

3. While the air fryer is Preheating, start the quick tomato sauce. Place the butter, garlic and red pepper flakes in a sauté pan and heat over medium heat on the stovetop. Let the garlic sizzle a little, but before the butter starts to brown, add the cinnamon and tomatoes. Bring to a simmer and simmer for 15 minutes. Season to taste with salt (but not too much as the feta that you will be sprinkling on at the end will be salty).

4. Brush the bottom of the air fryer basket with a little oil and transfer the meatballs to the air fryer basket in one layer, air-frying in batches if necessary.

5. Air-fry at 400°F for 8 minutes, giving the basket a shake once during the cooking process to turn the meatballs over.

6. To serve, spoon a pool of the tomato sauce onto plates and add the meatballs in a decorative manner. Sprinkle the feta cheese on top and garnish with more fresh parsley. Serve immediately.

Crispy Five-spice Pork Belly

Servings: 6   Cooking Time: 60-75 Minutes

Ingredients:

- 1½ pounds Pork belly with skin
- 3 tablespoons Shaoxing (Chinese cooking rice wine), dry sherry, or white grape juice
- 1½ teaspoons Granulated white sugar
- ¾ teaspoon Five-spice powder (see the headnote)
- 1¼ cups Coarse sea salt or kosher salt

Directions:

1. Preheat the air fryer to 350°F .

2. Set the pork belly skin side up on a cutting board. Use a meat fork to make dozens and dozens of tiny holes all across the surface of the skin. You can hardly make too many holes. These will allow the skin to bubble up and keep it from becoming hard as it roasts.

3. Turn the pork belly over so that one of its longer sides faces you. Make four evenly spaced vertical slits in the meat. The slits should go about halfway into the meat toward the fat.

4. Mix the Shaoxing or its substitute, sugar, and five-spice powder in a small bowl until the sugar dissolves. Massage this mixture across the meat and into the cuts.

5. Turn the pork belly over again. Blot dry any moisture on the skin. Make a double-thickness aluminum foil tray by setting two 10-inch-long pieces of foil on top of another. Set the pork belly skin side up in the center of this tray. Fold the sides of the tray up toward the pork, crimping the foil as you work to make a high-sided case all around the pork belly. Seal the foil to the meat on all sides so that only the skin is exposed.

6. Pour the salt onto the skin and pat it down and in place to create a crust. Pick up the foil tray with the pork in it and set it in the basket.

7. Air-fry undisturbed for 35 minutes for a small batch, 45 minutes for a medium batch, or 50 minutes for a large batch.

8. Remove the foil tray with the pork belly still in it. Warning: The foil tray is full of scalding-hot fat. Discard the fat in the tray (not down the drain!), as well as the tray itself. Transfer the pork belly to a cutting board.

9. Raise the air fryer temperature to 375°F (or 380°F or 390°F, if one of these is the closest setting). Brush the salt crust off the pork, removing any visible salt from the sides of the meat, too.

10. When the machine is at temperature, return the pork belly skin side up to the basket. Air-fry undisturbed for 25 minutes, or until crisp and very well browned. If the machine is at 390°F, you may be able to shave 5 minutes off the cooking time so that the skin doesn't blacken.

11. Use a nonstick-safe spatula, and perhaps a silicone baking mitt, to transfer the pork belly to a wire rack. Cool for 10 minutes before serving.

Garlic And Oregano Lamb Chops

Servings: 4

Cooking Time: 17 Minutes

Ingredients:

- ➤ 1½ tablespoons Olive oil
- ➤ 1 tablespoon Minced garlic
- ➤ 1 teaspoon Dried oregano
- ➤ 1 teaspoon Finely minced orange zest
- ➤ ¾ teaspoon Fennel seeds
- ➤ ¾ teaspoon Table salt
- ➤ ¾ teaspoon Ground black pepper
- ➤ 6 4-ounce, 1-inch-thick lamb loin chops

Directions:

1. Mix the olive oil, garlic, oregano, orange zest, fennel seeds, salt, and pepper in a large bowl. Add the chops and toss well to coat. Set aside as the air fryer heats, tossing one more time.

2. Preheat the air fryer to 400°F.

3. Set the chops bone side down in the basket (that is, so they stand up on their bony edge) with as much air space between them as possible. Air-fry undisturbed for 14 minutes for medium-rare, or until an instant-read meat thermometer inserted into the thickest part of a chop (without touching bone) registers 132°F (not USDA-approved). Or air-fry undisturbed for 17 minutes for well done, or until an instant-read meat thermometer registers 145°F (USDA-approved).

4. Use kitchen tongs to transfer the chops to a wire rack. Cool for 5 minutes before serving.

POULTRY RECIPES

Teriyaki Chicken Legs

Servings: 2

Cooking Time: 20 Minutes

Ingredients:

- ➢ 4 tablespoons teriyaki sauce
- ➢ 1 tablespoon orange juice
- ➢ 1 teaspoon smoked paprika
- ➢ 4 chicken legs
- ➢ cooking spray

Directions:

1. Mix together the teriyaki sauce, orange juice, and smoked paprika. Brush on all sides of chicken legs.
2. Spray air fryer basket with nonstick cooking spray and place chicken in basket.
3. Cook at 360°F for 6minutes. Turn and baste with sauce. Cook for 6 moreminutes, turn and baste.

Cook for 8 minutes more, until juices run clear when chicken is pierced with a fork.

Chicken Nuggets

Servings: 20

Cooking Time: 14 Minutes Per Batch

Ingredients:

- 1 pound boneless, skinless chicken thighs, cut into 1-inch chunks
- ¾ teaspoon salt
- ½ teaspoon black pepper
- ½ teaspoon garlic powder
- ½ teaspoon onion powder
- ½ cup flour
- 2 eggs, beaten
- ½ cup panko breadcrumbs
- 3 tablespoons plain breadcrumbs
- oil for misting or cooking spray

Directions:

1. In the bowl of a food processor, combine chicken, ½ teaspoon salt, pepper, garlic powder, and onion powder. Process in short pulses until chicken is very finely chopped and well blended.

2. Place flour in one shallow dish and beaten eggs in another. In a third dish or plastic bag, mix together the panko crumbs, plain breadcrumbs, and ¼ teaspoon salt.

3. Shape chicken mixture into small nuggets. Dip nuggets in flour, then eggs, then panko crumb mixture.

4. Spray nuggets on both sides with oil or cooking spray and place in air fryer basket in a single layer, close but not overlapping.

5. Cook at 360°F for 10minutes. Spray with oil and cook 4 minutes, until chicken is done and coating is golden brown.

6. Repeat step 5 to cook remaining nuggets.

Pickle Brined Fried Chicken

Servings: 4   Cooking Time: 47 Minutes

Ingredients:

- 4 bone-in, skin-on chicken legs, cut into drumsticks and thighs (about 3½ pounds)
- pickle juice from a 24-ounce jar of kosher dill pickles
- ½ cup flour
- salt and freshly ground black pepper
- 2 eggs
- 1 cup fine breadcrumbs
- 1 teaspoon salt
- 1 teaspoon freshly ground black pepper
- ½ teaspoon ground paprika
- ⅛ teaspoon ground cayenne pepper
- vegetable or canola oil in a spray bottle

Directions:

1. Place the chicken in a shallow dish and pour the pickle juice over the top. Cover and transfer the chicken to the refrigerator to brine in the pickle juice for 3 to 8 hours.

2. When you are ready to cook, remove the chicken from the refrigerator to let it come to room temperature while you set up a dredging station. Place the flour in a shallow dish and season well with salt and freshly ground black pepper. Whisk the eggs in a second shallow dish. In a third shallow dish, combine the breadcrumbs, salt, pepper, paprika and cayenne pepper.

3. Preheat the air fryer to 370°F.

4. Remove the chicken from the pickle brine and gently dry it with a clean kitchen towel. Dredge each piece of chicken in the flour, then dip it into the egg mixture, and finally press it into the breadcrumb mixture to coat all sides of the chicken. Place the breaded chicken on a plate or baking sheet and spray each piece all over with vegetable oil.

5. Air-fry the chicken in two batches. Place two chicken thighs and two drumsticks into the air fryer basket. Air-fry for 10 minutes. Then, gently turn the chicken pieces over and air-fry for another 10 minutes. Remove the chicken pieces and let them rest on plate – do not cover. Repeat with the second batch of chicken, air-frying for 20 minutes, turning the chicken over halfway through.

6. Lower the temperature of the air fryer to 340°F. Place the first batch of chicken on top of the second batch already in the basket and air-fry for an additional 7 minutes. Serve warm and enjoy.

Southern-fried Chicken Livers

Servings: 4

Cooking Time: 12 Minutes

Ingredients:

- 2 eggs
- 2 tablespoons water
- ¾ cup flour
- 1½ cups panko breadcrumbs
- ½ cup plain breadcrumbs
- 1 teaspoon salt
- ½ teaspoon black pepper
- 20 ounces chicken livers, salted to taste
- oil for misting or cooking spray

Directions:

1. Beat together eggs and water in a shallow dish. Place the flour in a separate shallow dish.

2. In the bowl of a food processor, combine the panko, plain breadcrumbs, salt, and pepper. Process until well mixed and panko crumbs are finely crushed. Place crumbs in a third shallow dish.

3. Dip livers in flour, then egg wash, and then roll in panko mixture to coat well with crumbs.

4. Spray both sides of livers with oil or cooking spray. Cooking in two batches, place livers in air fryer basket in single layer.

5. Cook at 390°F for 7minutes. Spray livers, turn over, and spray again. Cook for 5 more minutes, until done inside and coating is golden brown.

6. Repeat to cook remaining livers.

Parmesan Chicken Fingers

Servings: 2

Cooking Time: 19 Minutes

Ingredients:

- ½ cup flour
- 1 teaspoon salt
- freshly ground black pepper
- 2 eggs, beaten
- ¾ cup seasoned panko breadcrumbs
- ¾ cup grated Parmesan cheese
- 8 chicken tenders (about 1 pound)
- OR
- 2 to 3 boneless, skinless chicken breasts, cut into strips
- vegetable oil
- marinara sauce

Directions:

1. Set up a dredging station. Combine the flour, salt and pepper in a shallow dish. Place the beaten eggs in second shallow dish, and combine the panko breadcrumbs and Parmesan cheese in a third shallow dish.

2. Dredge the chicken tenders in the flour mixture. Then dip them into the egg, and finally place the chicken in the breadcrumb mixture. Press the coating onto both sides of the chicken tenders. Place the coated chicken tenders on a baking sheet until they are all coated. Spray both sides of the chicken fingers with vegetable oil.

3. Preheat the air fryer to 360°F.

4. Air-fry the chicken fingers in two batches. Transfer half the chicken fingers to the air fryer basket and air-fry for 9 minutes, turning the chicken over halfway through the cooking time. When the second batch of chicken fingers has finished cooking, return the first batch to the air fryer with the second batch and air-fry for one minute to heat everything through.

5. Serve immediately with marinara sauce, honey-mustard, ketchup or your favorite dipping sauce.

Peanut Butter-barbeque Chicken

Servings: 4

Cooking Time: 20 Minutes

Ingredients:

- 1 pound boneless, skinless chicken thighs
- salt and pepper
- 1 large orange
- ½ cup barbeque sauce
- 2 tablespoons smooth peanut butter
- 2 tablespoons chopped peanuts for garnish (optional)
- cooking spray

Directions:

1. Season chicken with salt and pepper to taste. Place in a shallow dish or plastic bag.

2. Grate orange peel, squeeze orange and reserve 1 tablespoon of juice for the sauce.

3. Pour remaining juice over chicken and marinate for 30minutes.

4. Mix together the reserved 1 tablespoon of orange juice, barbeque sauce, peanut butter, and 1 teaspoon grated orange peel.

5. Place ¼ cup of sauce mixture in a small bowl for basting. Set remaining sauce aside to serve with cooked chicken.

6. Preheat air fryer to 360°F. Spray basket with nonstick cooking spray.

7. Remove chicken from marinade, letting excess drip off. Place in air fryer basket and cook for 5minutes. Turn chicken over and cook 5minutes longer.

8. Brush both sides of chicken lightly with sauce.

9. Cook chicken 5minutes, then turn thighs one more time, again brushing both sides lightly with sauce. Cook for 5 moreminutes or until chicken is done and juices run clear.

10. Serve chicken with remaining sauce on the side and garnish with chopped peanuts if you like.

Southern-style Chicken Legs

Servings: 6

Cooking Time: 20 Minutes

Ingredients:

- 2 cups buttermilk
- 1 tablespoon hot sauce
- 12 chicken legs
- ½ teaspoon salt
- ½ teaspoon pepper
- 1 teaspoon paprika
- ½ teaspoon onion powder
- 1 teaspoon garlic powder
- 1 cup all-purpose flour

Directions:

1. In an airtight container, place the buttermilk, hot sauce, and chicken legs and refrigerate for 4 to 8 hours.

2. In a medium bowl, whisk together the salt, pepper, paprika, onion powder, garlic powder, and flour. Drain the chicken legs from the buttermilk and dip the chicken legs into the flour mixture, stirring to coat well.

3. Preheat the air fryer to 390°F.

4. Place the chicken legs in the air fryer basket and spray with cooking spray. Cook for 10 minutes, turn the chicken legs over, and cook for another 8 to 10 minutes. Check for an internal temperature of 165°F.

Chicken Cordon Bleu

Servings: 2

Cooking Time: 16 Minutes

Ingredients:

- ➢ 2 boneless, skinless chicken breasts
- ➢ ¼ teaspoon salt
- ➢ 2 teaspoons Dijon mustard
- ➢ 2 ounces deli ham
- ➢ 2 ounces Swiss, fontina, or Gruyère cheese
- ➢ ⅓ cup all-purpose flour
- ➢ 1 egg
- ➢ ½ cup breadcrumbs

Directions:

1. Pat the chicken breasts with a paper towel. Season the chicken with the salt. Pound the chicken breasts to 1½ inches thick. Create a pouch by slicing the side of each chicken breast. Spread 1 teaspoon Dijon mustard inside the pouch of each chicken breast. Wrap a 1-ounce slice of ham around a 1-ounce slice of cheese and place into the pouch. Repeat with the remaining ham and cheese.

2. In a medium bowl, place the flour.

3. In a second bowl, whisk the egg.

4. In a third bowl, place the breadcrumbs.

5. Dredge the chicken in the flour and shake off the excess. Next, dip the chicken into the egg and then in the breadcrumbs. Set the chicken on a plate and repeat with the remaining chicken piece.

6. Preheat the air fryer to 360°F.

7. Place the chicken in the air fryer basket and spray liberally with cooking spray. Cook for 8 minutes, turn the chicken breasts over, and liberally spray with cooking spray again; cook another 6 minutes. Once golden brown, check for an internal temperature of 165°F.

Cornish Hens With Honey-lime Glaze

Servings: 2

Cooking Time: 30 Minutes

Ingredients:

- 1 Cornish game hen (1½–2 pounds)
- 1 tablespoon honey
- 1 tablespoon lime juice
- 1 teaspoon poultry seasoning
- salt and pepper
- cooking spray

Directions:

1. To split the hen into halves, cut through breast bone and down one side of the backbone.

2. Mix the honey, lime juice, and poultry seasoning together and brush or rub onto all sides of the hen. Season to taste with salt and pepper.

3. Spray air fryer basket with cooking spray and place hen halves in the basket, skin-side down.

4. Cook at 330°F for 30 minutes. Hen will be done when juices run clear when pierced at leg joint with a fork. Let hen rest for 5 to 10minutes before cutting.

Buffalo Egg Rolls

Servings: 8   Cooking Time: 9 Minutes Per Batch

Ingredients:

- 1 teaspoon water
- 1 tablespoon cornstarch
- 1 egg
- 2½ cups cooked chicken, diced or shredded (see opposite page)
- ⅓ cup chopped green onion
- ⅓ cup diced celery
- ⅓ cup buffalo wing sauce
- 8 egg roll wraps
- oil for misting or cooking spray
- Blue Cheese Dip
- 3 ounces cream cheese, softened
- ⅓ cup blue cheese, crumbled
- 1 teaspoon Worcestershire sauce
- ¼ teaspoon garlic powder
- ¼ cup buttermilk (or sour cream)

Directions:

1. Mix water and cornstarch in a small bowl until dissolved. Add egg, beat well, and set aside.
2. In a medium size bowl, mix together chicken, green onion, celery, and buffalo wing sauce.
3. Divide chicken mixture evenly among 8 egg roll wraps, spooning ½ inch from one edge.
4. Moisten all edges of each wrap with beaten egg wash.
5. Fold the short ends over filling, then roll up tightly and press to seal edges.
6. Brush outside of wraps with egg wash, then spritz with oil or cooking spray.
7. Place 4 egg rolls in air fryer basket.
8. Cook at 390°F for 9minutes or until outside is brown and crispy.
9. While the rolls are cooking, prepare the Blue Cheese Dip. With a fork, mash together cream cheese and blue cheese.
10. Stir in remaining ingredients.
11. Dip should be just thick enough to slightly cling to egg rolls. If too thick, stir in buttermilk or milk 1 tablespoon at a time until you reach the desired consistency.
12. Cook remaining 4 egg rolls as in steps 7 and 8.
13. Serve while hot with Blue Cheese Dip, more buffalo wing sauce, or both.

Crispy Duck With Cherry Sauce

Servings: 2   Cooking Time: 33 Minutes

Ingredients:

- 1 whole duck (up to 5 pounds), split in half, back and rib bones removed
- 1 teaspoon olive oil
- salt and freshly ground black pepper
- Cherry Sauce:
- 1 tablespoon butter
- 1 shallot, minced
- ½ cup sherry
- ¾ cup cherry preserves 1 cup chicken stock
- 1 teaspoon white wine vinegar
- 1 teaspoon fresh thyme leaves
- salt and freshly ground black pepper

Directions:

1. Preheat the air fryer to 400°F.

2. Trim some of the fat from the duck. Rub olive oil on the duck and season with salt and pepper. Place the duck halves in the air fryer basket, breast side up and facing the center of the basket.

3. Air-fry the duck for 20 minutes. Turn the duck over and air-fry for another 6 minutes.

4. While duck is air-frying, make the cherry sauce. Melt the butter in a large sauté pan. Add the shallot and sauté until it is just starting to brown – about 2 to 3 minutes. Add the sherry and deglaze the pan by scraping up any brown bits from the bottom of the pan. Simmer the liquid for a few minutes, until it has reduced by half. Add the cherry preserves, chicken stock and white wine vinegar. Whisk well to combine all the ingredients. Simmer the sauce until it thickens and coats the back of a spoon – about 5 to 7 minutes. Season with salt and pepper and stir in the fresh thyme leaves.

5. When the air fryer timer goes off, spoon some cherry sauce over the duck and continue to air-fry at 400°F for 4 more minutes. Then, turn the duck halves back over so that the breast side is facing up. Spoon more cherry sauce over the top of the duck, covering the skin completely. Air-fry for 3 more minutes and then remove the duck to a plate to rest for a few minutes.

6. Serve the duck in halves, or cut each piece in half again for a smaller serving. Spoon any additional sauce over the duck or serve it on the side.

Chicken Wellington

Servings: 2	Cooking Time: 31 Minutes

Ingredients:

- 2 (5-ounce) boneless, skinless chicken breasts
- ½ cup White Worcestershire sauce
- 3 tablespoons butter
- ½ cup finely diced onion (about ½ onion)
- 8 ounces button mushrooms, finely chopped
- ¼ cup chicken stock
- 2 tablespoons White Worcestershire sauce (or white wine)
- salt and freshly ground black pepper
- 1 tablespoon chopped fresh tarragon
- 2 sheets puff pastry, thawed
- 1 egg, beaten
- vegetable oil

Directions:

1. Place the chicken breasts in a shallow dish. Pour the White Worcestershire sauce over the chicken coating both sides and marinate for 30 minutes.

2. While the chicken is marinating, melt the butter in a large skillet over medium-high heat on the stovetop. Add the onion and sauté for a few minutes, until it starts to soften. Add the mushrooms and sauté for 5 minutes until the vegetables are brown and soft. Deglaze the skillet with the chicken stock, scraping up any bits from the bottom of the pan. Add the White Worcestershire sauce and simmer for 3 minutes until the mixture reduces and starts to thicken. Season with salt and freshly ground black pepper. Remove the mushroom mixture from the heat and stir in the fresh tarragon. Let the mushroom mixture cool.

3. Preheat the air fryer to 360°F.

4. Remove the chicken from the marinade and transfer it to the air fryer basket. Tuck the small end of the chicken breast under the thicker part to shape it into a circle rather than an oval. Pour the marinade over the chicken and air-fry for 10 minutes.

5. Roll out the puff pastry and cut out two 6-inch squares. Brush the perimeter of each square with the egg wash. Place half of the mushroom mixture in the center of each puff pastry square. Place the chicken breasts, top side down on the mushroom mixture. Starting with one corner of puff pastry and working in one direction, pull the pastry up over the chicken to enclose it and press the ends of the pastry together

in the middle. Brush the pastry with the egg wash to seal the edges. Turn the Wellingtons over and set aside.

6.   To make a decorative design with the remaining puff pastry, cut out four 10-inch strips. For each Wellington, twist two of the strips together, place them over the chicken breast wrapped in puff pastry, and tuck the ends underneath to seal it. Brush the entire top and sides of the Wellingtons with the egg wash.

7.   Preheat the air fryer to 350°F.

8.   Spray or brush the air fryer basket with vegetable oil. Air-fry the chicken Wellingtons for 13 minutes. Carefully turn the Wellingtons over. Air-fry for another 8 minutes. Transfer to serving plates, light a candle and enjoy!

APPETIZERS AND SNACKS

Crispy Spiced Chickpeas

Servings: 2

Cooking Time: 20 Minutes

Ingredients:

➢ 1 (15-ounce) can chickpeas, drained (or 1½ cups cooked chickpeas)

➢ ½ teaspoon salt

➢ ½ teaspoon chili powder

➢ ¼ teaspoon ground cinnamon

➢ ⅛ teaspoon smoked paprika

➢ pinch ground cayenne pepper

➢ 1 tablespoon olive oil

Directions:

1. Preheat the air fryer to 400°F.

2. Dry the chickpeas as well as you can with a clean kitchen towel, rubbing off any loose skins as necessary. Combine the spices in a small bowl. Toss the chickpeas with the olive oil and then add the spices and toss again.

3. Air-fry for 15 minutes, shaking the basket a couple of times while they cook.

4. Check the chickpeas to see if they are crispy enough and if necessary, air-fry for another 5 minutes to crisp them further. Serve warm, or cool to room temperature and store in an airtight container for up to two weeks.

Loaded Potato Skins

Servings: 8

Cooking Time: 8 Minutes

Ingredients:

- ➤ 12 round baby potatoes
- ➤ 3 ounces cream cheese
- ➤ 4 slices cooked bacon, crumbled or chopped
- ➤ 2 green onions, finely chopped
- ➤ ½ cup grated cheddar cheese, divided
- ➤ ¼ cup sour cream
- ➤ 1 tablespoon milk
- ➤ 2 teaspoons hot sauce

Directions:

1. Preheat the air fryer to 320°F.

2. Poke holes into the baby potatoes with a fork. Place the potatoes onto a microwave-safe plate and microwave on high for 4 to 5 minutes, or until soft to squeeze. Let the potatoes cool until they're safe to handle, about 5 minutes.

3. Meanwhile, in a medium bowl, mix together the cream cheese, bacon, green onions, and ¼ cup of the cheddar cheese; set aside.

4. Slice the baby potatoes in half. Using a spoon, scoop out the pulp, leaving enough pulp on the inside to retain the shape of the potato half. Place the potato pulp into the cream cheese mixture and mash together with a fork. Using a spoon, refill the potato halves with filling.

5. Place the potato halves into the air fryer basket and top with the remaining ¼ cup of cheddar cheese.

6. Cook the loaded baked potato bites in batches for 8 minutes.

7. Meanwhile, make the sour cream sauce. In a small bowl, whisk together the sour cream, milk, and hot sauce. Add more hot sauce if desired.

8. When the potatoes have all finished cooking, place them onto a serving platter and serve with sour cream sauce drizzled over the top or as a dip.

Green Olive And Mushroom Tapenade

Servings: 1

Cooking Time: 10 Minutes

Ingredients:

- ¾ pound Brown or Baby Bella mushrooms, sliced
- 1½ cups (about ½ pound) Pitted green olives
- 3 tablespoons Olive oil
- 1½ tablespoons Fresh oregano leaves, loosely packed
- ¼ teaspoon Ground black pepper

Directions:

1. Preheat the air fryer to 400°F.

2. When the machine is at temperature, arrange the mushroom slices in as close to an even layer as possible in the basket. They will overlap and even stack on top of each other.

3. Air-fry for 10 minutes, tossing the basket and rearranging the mushrooms every 2 minutes, until shriveled but with still-noticeable moisture.

4. Pour the mushrooms into a food processor. Add the olives, olive oil, oregano leaves, and pepper. Cover and process until grainy, not too much, just not fully smooth for better texture, stopping the machine at least once to scrape down the inside of the canister. Scrape the tapenade into a bowl and serve warm, or cover and refrigerate for up to 4 days. (The tapenade will taste better if it comes back to room temperature before serving.)

Cauliflower "tater" Tots

Servings: 6

Cooking Time: 10 Minutes

Ingredients:

- 1 head of cauliflower
- 2 eggs
- ¼ cup all-purpose flour*
- ½ cup grated Parmesan cheese
- 1 teaspoon salt
- freshly ground black pepper
- vegetable or olive oil, in a spray bottle

Directions:

1. Grate the head of cauliflower with a box grater or finely chop it in a food processor. You should have about 3½ cups. Place the chopped cauliflower in the center of a clean kitchen towel and twist the towel tightly to squeeze all the water out of the cauliflower. (This can be done in two batches to make it easier to drain all the water from the cauliflower.)

2. Place the squeezed cauliflower in a large bowl. Add the eggs, flour, Parmesan cheese, salt and freshly ground black pepper. Shape the cauliflower into small cylinders or "tater tot" shapes, rolling roughly one tablespoon of the mixture at a time. Place the tots on a cookie sheet lined with paper towel to absorb any residual moisture. Spray the cauliflower tots all over with oil.

3. Preheat the air fryer to 400°F.

4. Air-fry the tots at 400°F, one layer at a time for 10 minutes, turning them over for the last few minutes of the cooking process for even browning. Season with salt and black pepper. Serve hot with your favorite dipping sauce.

Individual Pizzas

Servings: 2

Cooking Time: 7 Minutes

Ingredients:

➢ 6 ounces Purchased fresh pizza dough (not a prebaked crust)

➢ Olive oil spray

➢ 4½ tablespoons Purchased pizza sauce or purchased pesto

➢ ½ cup (about 2 ounces) Shredded semi-firm mozzarella

Directions:

1. Preheat the air fryer to 400°F.

2. Press the pizza dough into a 5-inch circle for a small air fryer, a 6-inch circle for a medium air fryer, or a 7-inch circle for a large machine. Generously coat the top of the dough with olive oil spray.

3. Remove the basket from the machine and set the dough oil side down in the basket. Smear the sauce or pesto over the dough, then sprinkle with the cheese.

4. Return the basket to the machine and air-fry undisturbed for 7 minutes, or until the dough is puffed and browned and the cheese has melted. (Extra toppings will not increase the cooking time, provided you add no extra cheese.)

5. Remove the basket from the machine and cool the pizza in it for 5 minutes. Use a large nonstick-safe spatula to transfer the pizza from the basket to a wire rack. Cool for 5 minutes more before serving.

Crispy Wontons

Servings: 8   Cooking Time: 10 Minutes

Ingredients:

- ½ cup refried beans
- 3 tablespoons salsa
- ¼ cup canned artichoke hearts, drained and patted dry
- ¼ cup frozen spinach, defrosted and squeezed dry
- 2 ounces cream cheese
- 1½ teaspoons dried oregano, divided
- ¼ teaspoon garlic powder
- ¼ teaspoon onion powder
- ½ teaspoon salt
- ¼ cup chopped pepperoni
- ¼ cup grated mozzarella cheese
- 1 tablespoon grated Parmesan
- 2 ounces cream cheese
- ½ teaspoon dried oregano
- 32 wontons
- 1 cup water

Directions:

1. Preheat the air fryer to 370°F.

2. In a medium bowl, mix together the refried beans and salsa.

3. In a second medium bowl, mix together the artichoke hearts, spinach, cream cheese, oregano, garlic powder, onion powder, and salt.

4. In a third medium bowl, mix together the pepperoni, mozzarella cheese, Parmesan cheese, cream cheese, and the remaining ½ teaspoon of oregano.

5. Get a towel lightly damp with water and ring it out. While working with the wontons, leave the unfilled wontons under the damp towel so they don't dry out.

6. Working with 8 wontons at a time, place 2 teaspoons of one of the fillings into the center of the wonton, rotating among the different fillings (one filling per wonton). Working one at a time, use a pastry brush, dip the pastry brush into the water, and brush the edges of the dough with the water. Fold the dough in half to form a triangle and set aside. Continue until 8 wontons are formed. Spray the wontons with cooking spray and cover with a dry towel. Repeat until all 32 wontons have been filled.

7. Place the wontons into the air fryer basket, leaving space between the wontons, and cook for 5 minutes. Turn over and check for brownness, and then cook for another 5 minutes.

Avocado Fries, Vegan

Servings: 4

Cooking Time: 10 Minutes

Ingredients:

- ¼ cup almond or coconut milk
- 1 tablespoon lime juice
- ⅛ teaspoon hot sauce
- 2 tablespoons flour
- ¾ cup panko breadcrumbs
- ¼ cup cornmeal
- ¼ teaspoon salt
- 1 large avocado
- oil for misting or cooking spray

Directions:

1. In a small bowl, whisk together the almond or coconut milk, lime juice, and hot sauce.
2. Place flour on a sheet of wax paper.
3. Mix panko, cornmeal, and salt and place on another sheet of wax paper.
4. Split avocado in half and remove pit. Peel or use a spoon to lift avocado halves out of the skin.
5. Cut avocado lengthwise into ½-inch slices. Dip each in flour, then milk mixture, then roll in panko mixture.
6. Mist with oil or cooking spray and cook at 390°F for 10minutes, until crust is brown and crispy.

Buffalo Bites

Servings: 16

Cooking Time: 12 Minutes

Ingredients:

- ➢ 1 pound ground chicken
- ➢ 8 tablespoons buffalo wing sauce
- ➢ 2 ounces Gruyère cheese, cut into 16 cubes
- ➢ 1 tablespoon maple syrup

Directions:

1. Mix 4 tablespoons buffalo wing sauce into all the ground chicken.
2. Shape chicken into a log and divide into 16 equal portions.
3. With slightly damp hands, mold each chicken portion around a cube of cheese and shape into a firm ball. When you have shaped 8 meatballs, place them in air fryer basket.
4. Cook at 390°F for approximately 5minutes. Shake basket, reduce temperature to 360°F, and cook for 5 minutes longer.
5. While the first batch is cooking, shape remaining chicken and cheese into 8 more meatballs.
6. Repeat step 4 to cook second batch of meatballs.
7. In a medium bowl, mix the remaining 4 tablespoons of buffalo wing sauce with the maple syrup. Add all the cooked meatballs and toss to coat.
8. Place meatballs back into air fryer basket and cook at 390°F for 2 minutes to set the glaze. Skewer each with a toothpick and serve.

Avocado Fries With Quick Salsa Fresca

Ingredients:

- ½ cup flour*
- 2 teaspoons salt
- 2 eggs, lightly beaten
- 1 cup panko breadcrumbs*
- ⅛ teaspoon cayenne pepper
- ¼ teaspoon smoked paprika (optional)
- 2 large avocados, just ripe
- vegetable oil, in a spray bottle

- Quick Salsa Fresca
- 1 cup cherry tomatoes
- 1 tablespoon-sized chunk of shallot or red onion
- 2 teaspoons fresh lime juice
- 1 teaspoon chopped fresh cilantro or parsley
- salt and freshly ground black pepper

Directions:

1. Set up a dredging station with three shallow dishes. Place the flour and salt in the first shallow dish. Place the eggs into the second dish. Combine the breadcrumbs, cayenne pepper and paprika (if using) in the third dish.

2. Preheat the air fryer to 400°F.

3. Cut the avocado in half around the pit and separate the two sides. Slice the avocados into long strips while still in their skin. Run a spoon around the slices, separating them from the avocado skin. Try to keep the slices whole, but don't worry if they break – you can still coat and air-fry the pieces.

4. Coat the avocado slices by dredging them first in the flour, then the egg and then the breadcrumbs, pressing the crumbs on gently with your hands. Set the coated avocado fries on a tray and spray them on all sides with vegetable oil.

5. Air-fry the avocado fries, one layer at a time, at 400°F for 6 minutes, turning them over halfway through the cooking time and spraying lightly again if necessary. When the fries are nicely browned on all sides, season with salt and remove.

6. While the avocado fries are air-frying, make the salsa fresca by combining everything in a food processor. Pulse several times until the salsa is a chunky purée. Serve the fries warm with the salsa on the side for dipping.

Antipasto-stuffed Cherry Tomatoes

Servings: 12

Cooking Time: 9 Minutes

Ingredients:

➢ 12 Large cherry tomatoes, preferably Campari tomatoes (about 1½ ounces each and the size of golf balls)

➢ ½ cup Seasoned Italian-style dried bread crumbs (gluten-free, if a concern)

➢ ¼ cup (about ¾ ounce) Finely grated Parmesan cheese

➢ ¼ cup Finely chopped pitted black olives

➢ ¼ cup Finely chopped marinated artichoke hearts

➢ 2 tablespoons Marinade from the artichokes

➢ 4 Sun-dried tomatoes (dry, not packed in oil), finely chopped

➢ Olive oil spray

Directions:

1. Preheat the air fryer to 400°F.

2. Cut the top off of each fresh tomato, exposing the seeds and pulp. (The tops can be saved for a snack, sprinkled with some kosher salt, to tide you over while the stuffed tomatoes cook.) Cut a very small slice off the bottom of each tomato (no cutting into the pulp) so it will stand up flat on your work surface. Use a melon baller to remove and discard the seeds and pulp from each tomato.

3. Mix the bread crumbs, cheese, olives, artichoke hearts, marinade, and sun-dried tomatoes in a bowl until well combined. Stuff this mixture into each prepared tomato, about 1½ tablespoons in each. Generously coat the tops of the tomatoes with olive oil spray.

4. Set the tomatoes stuffing side up in the basket. Air-fry undisturbed for 9 minutes, or until the stuffing has browned a bit and the tomatoes are blistered in places.

5. Remove the basket and cool the tomatoes in it for 5 minutes. Then use kitchen tongs to gently transfer the tomatoes to a serving platter.

Crunchy Spicy Chickpeas

Servings: 6

Cooking Time: 12 Minutes

Ingredients:

- 2½ cups Canned chickpeas, drained and rinsed
- 2½ tablespoons Vegetable or canola oil
- up to 1 tablespoon Cajun or jerk dried seasoning blend (see here for a Cajun blend, here for a jerk blend)
- up to ¾ teaspoon Table salt (optional)

Directions:

1. Preheat the air fryer to 400°F.

2. Toss the chickpeas, oil, seasoning blend, and salt (if using) in a large bowl until the chickpeas are evenly coated.

3. When the machine is at temperature, pour the chickpeas into the basket. Air-fry for 12 minutes, removing the basket at the 4- and 8-minute marks to toss and rearrange the chickpeas, until very aromatic and perhaps sizzling but not burned.

4. Pour the chickpeas into a large serving bowl. Cool for a couple of minutes, gently stirring once, before you dive in.

Garlic Wings

Servings: 4

Cooking Time: 15 Minutes

Ingredients:

- 2 pounds chicken wings
- oil for misting
- cooking spray
- Marinade
- 1 cup buttermilk
- 2 cloves garlic, mashed flat
- 1 teaspoon Worcestershire sauce
- 1 bay leaf
- Coating
- 1½ cups grated Parmesan cheese
- ¾ cup breadcrumbs
- 1½ tablespoons garlic powder
- ½ teaspoon salt

Directions:

1. Mix all marinade ingredients together.
2. Remove wing tips (the third joint) and discard or freeze for stock. Cut the remaining wings at the joint and toss them into the marinade, stirring to coat well. Refrigerate for at least an hour but no more than 8 hours.
3. When ready to cook, combine all coating ingredients in a shallow dish.
4. Remove wings from marinade, shaking off excess, and roll in coating mixture. Press coating into wings so that it sticks well. Spray wings with oil.
5. Spray air fryer basket with cooking spray. Place wings in basket in single layer, close but not touching.
6. Cook at 360°F for 15minutes or until chicken is done and juices run clear.
7. Repeat previous step to cook remaining wings.

VEGETABLE SIDE DISHES RECIPES

Fried Eggplant Balls

Servings: 4   Cooking Time: 40 Minutes

Ingredients:

- 1 medium eggplant (about 1 pound)
- olive oil
- salt and freshly ground black pepper
- 1 cup grated Parmesan cheese
- 2 cups fresh breadcrumbs
- 2 tablespoons chopped fresh parsley
- 2 tablespoons chopped fresh basil
- 1 clove garlic, minced
- 1 egg, lightly beaten
- ½ cup fine dried breadcrumbs

Directions:

1. Preheat the air fryer to 400°F.

2. Quarter the eggplant by cutting it in half both lengthwise and horizontally. Make a few slashes in the flesh of the eggplant but not through the skin. Brush the cut surface of the eggplant generously with olive oil and transfer to the air fryer basket, cut side up. Air-fry for 10 minutes. Turn the eggplant quarters cut side down and air-fry for another 15 minutes or until the eggplant is soft all the way through. You may need to rotate the pieces in the air fryer so that they cook evenly. Transfer the eggplant to a cutting board to cool.

3. Place the Parmesan cheese, the fresh breadcrumbs, fresh herbs, garlic and egg in a food processor. Scoop the flesh out of the eggplant, discarding the skin and any pieces that are tough. You should have about 1 to 1½ cups of eggplant. Add the eggplant to the food processor and process everything together until smooth. Season with salt and pepper. Refrigerate the mixture for at least 30 minutes.

4. Place the dried breadcrumbs into a shallow dish or onto a plate. Scoop heaping tablespoons of the eggplant mixture into the dried breadcrumbs. Roll the dollops of eggplant in the breadcrumbs and then shape into small balls. You should have 16 to 18 eggplant balls at the end. Refrigerate until you are ready to air-fry.

5. Preheat the air fryer to 350°F.

6. Spray the eggplant balls and the air fryer basket with olive oil. Air-fry the eggplant balls for 15 minutes, rotating the balls during the cooking process to brown evenly.

Fried Pearl Onions With Balsamic Vinegar And Basil

Servings: 2

Cooking Time: 10 Minutes

Ingredients:

- 1 pound fresh pearl onions
- 1 tablespoon olive oil
- salt and freshly ground black pepper
- 1 teaspoon high quality aged balsamic vinegar
- 1 tablespoon chopped fresh basil leaves (or mint)

Directions:

1. Preheat the air fryer to 400°F.

2. Decide whether you want to peel the onions before or after they cook. Peeling them ahead of time is a little more laborious. Peeling after they cook is easier, but a little messier since the onions are hot and you may discard more of the onion than you'd like to. If you opt to peel them first, trim the tiny root of the onions off and pinch off any loose papery skins. (It's ok if there are some skins left on the onions.) Toss the pearl onions with the olive oil, salt and freshly ground black pepper.

3. Air-fry for 10 minutes, shaking the basket a couple of times during the cooking process. (If your pearl onions are very large, you may need to add a couple of minutes to this cooking time.)

4. Let the onions cool slightly and then slip off any remaining skins.

5. Toss the onions with the balsamic vinegar and basil and serve.

Blistered Tomatoes

Servings: 20

Cooking Time: 15 Minutes

Ingredients:

- 1½ pounds Cherry or grape tomatoes
- Olive oil spray
- 1½ teaspoons Balsamic vinegar
- ¼ teaspoon Table salt
- ¼ teaspoon Ground black pepper

Directions:

1. Put the basket in a drawer-style air fryer, or a baking tray in the lower third of a toaster oven–style air fryer. Place a 6-inch round cake pan in the basket or on the tray for a small batch, a 7-inch round cake pan for a medium batch, or an 8-inch round cake pan for a large one. Heat the air fryer to 400°F with the pan in the basket. When the machine is at temperature, keep heating the pan for 5 minutes more.

2. Place the tomatoes in a large bowl, coat them with the olive oil spray, toss gently, then spritz a couple of times more, tossing after each spritz, until the tomatoes are glistening.

3. Pour the tomatoes into the cake pan and air-fry undisturbed for 10 minutes, or until they split and begin to brown.

4. Use kitchen tongs and a nonstick-safe spatula, or silicone baking mitts, to remove the cake pan from the basket. Toss the hot tomatoes with the vinegar, salt, and pepper. Cool in the pan for a few minutes before serving.

Cauliflower

Servings: 4

Cooking Time: 6 Minutes

Ingredients:

- ½ cup water
- 1 10-ounce package frozen cauliflower (florets)
- 1 teaspoon lemon pepper seasoning

Directions:

1. Pour the water into air fryer drawer.
2. Pour the frozen cauliflower into the air fryer basket and sprinkle with lemon pepper seasoning.
3. Cook at 390°F for approximately 6 minutes.

Fried Okra

Servings: 4

Cooking Time: 8 Minutes

Ingredients:

- ➢ 1 pound okra
- ➢ 1 large egg
- ➢ 1 tablespoon milk
- ➢ 1 teaspoon salt, divided
- ➢ ½ teaspoon black pepper, divided
- ➢ ¼ teaspoon paprika
- ➢ ¼ teaspoon thyme
- ➢ ½ cup cornmeal
- ➢ ½ cup all-purpose flour

Directions:

1. Preheat the air fryer to 400°F.

2. Cut the okra into ½-inch rounds.

3. In a medium bowl, whisk together the egg, milk, ½ teaspoon of the salt, and ¼ teaspoon of black pepper. Place the okra into the egg mixture and toss until well coated.

4. In a separate bowl, mix together the remaining ½ teaspoon of salt, the remaining ¼ teaspoon of black pepper, the paprika, the thyme, the cornmeal, and the flour. Working in small batches, dredge the egg-coated okra in the cornmeal mixture until all the okra has been breaded.

5. Place a single layer of okra in the air fryer basket and spray with cooking spray. Cook for 4 minutes, toss to check for crispness, and cook another 4 minutes. Repeat in batches, as needed.

Grits Casserole

Servings: 4

Cooking Time: 30 Minutes

Ingredients:

➢ 10 fresh asparagus spears, cut into 1-inch pieces

➢ 2 cups cooked grits, cooled to room temperature

➢ 1 egg, beaten

➢ 2 teaspoons Worcestershire sauce

➢ ½ teaspoon garlic powder

➢ ¼ teaspoon salt

➢ 2 slices provolone cheese (about 1½ ounces)

➢ oil for misting or cooking spray

Directions:

1. Mist asparagus spears with oil and cook at 390°F for 5minutes, until crisp-tender.

2. In a medium bowl, mix together the grits, egg, Worcestershire, garlic powder, and salt.

3. Spoon half of grits mixture into air fryer baking pan and top with asparagus.

4. Tear cheese slices into pieces and layer evenly on top of asparagus.

5. Top with remaining grits.

6. Bake at 360°F for 25 minutes. The casserole will rise a little as it cooks. When done, the top will have browned lightly with just a hint of crispiness.

Tuna Platter

Servings: 4

Cooking Time: 9 Minutes

Ingredients:

- 4 new potatoes, boiled in their jackets
- ½ cup vinaigrette dressing, plus 2 tablespoons
- ½ pound fresh green beans, cut in half-inch pieces and steamed
- 1 tablespoon Herbes de Provence
- 1 tablespoon minced shallots
- 1½ tablespoons tarragon vinegar
- 4 tuna steaks, each ¾-inch thick, about 1 pound
- salt and pepper
- Salad
- 8 cups chopped romaine lettuce
- 12 grape tomatoes, halved lengthwise
- ½ cup pitted olives (black, green, nicoise, or combination)
- 2 boiled eggs, peeled and halved lengthwise

Directions:

1. Quarter potatoes and toss with 1 tablespoon salad dressing.

2. Toss the warm beans with the other tablespoon of salad dressing. Set both aside while you prepare the tuna.

3. Mix together the herbs, shallots, and vinegar and rub into all sides of tuna. Season fish to taste with salt and pepper.

4. Cook tuna at 390°F for 7minutes and check. If needed, cook 2 minutes longer, until tuna is barely pink in the center.

5. Spread the lettuce over a large platter.

6. Slice the tuna steaks in ½-inch pieces and arrange them in the center of the lettuce.

7. Place the remaining ingredients around the tuna. Diners create their own plates by selecting what they want from the platter. Pass remainder of salad dressing at the table.

Hasselbacks

Servings: 4

Cooking Time: 41 Minutes

Ingredients:

- 2 large potatoes (approx. 1 pound each)
- oil for misting or cooking spray
- salt, pepper, and garlic powder
- 1½ ounces sharp Cheddar cheese, sliced very thin
- ¼ cup chopped green onions
- 2 strips turkey bacon, cooked and crumbled
- light sour cream for serving (optional)

Directions:

1. Preheat air fryer to 390°F.

2. Scrub potatoes. Cut thin vertical slices ¼-inch thick crosswise about three-quarters of the way down so that bottom of potato remains intact.

3. Fan potatoes slightly to separate slices. Mist with oil and sprinkle with salt, pepper, and garlic powder to taste. Potatoes will be very stiff, but try to get some of the oil and seasoning between the slices.

4. Place potatoes in air fryer basket and cook for 40 minutes or until centers test done when pierced with a fork.

5. Top potatoes with cheese slices and cook for 30 seconds to 1 minute to melt cheese.

6. Cut each potato in half crosswise, and sprinkle with green onions and crumbled bacon. If you like, add a dollop of sour cream before serving.

Sweet Potato Fries

Servings: 4

Cooking Time: 30 Minutes

Ingredients:

- ➢ 2 pounds sweet potatoes
- ➢ 1 teaspoon dried marjoram
- ➢ 2 teaspoons olive oil
- ➢ sea salt

Directions:

1. Peel and cut the potatoes into ¼-inch sticks, 4 to 5 inches long.

2. In a sealable plastic bag or bowl with lid, toss sweet potatoes with marjoram and olive oil. Rub seasonings in to coat well.

3. Pour sweet potatoes into air fryer basket and cook at 390°F for approximately 30 minutes, until cooked through with some brown spots on edges.

4. Season to taste with sea salt.

Buttery Rolls

Servings: 6	Cooking Time: 14 Minutes

Ingredients:

- 6½ tablespoons Room-temperature whole or low-fat milk
- 3 tablespoons plus 1 teaspoon Butter, melted and cooled
- 3 tablespoons plus 1 teaspoon (or 1 medium egg, well beaten) Pasteurized egg substitute, such as Egg Beaters
- 1½ tablespoons Granulated white sugar
- 1¼ teaspoons Instant yeast
- ¼ teaspoon Table salt
- 2 cups, plus more for dusting All-purpose flour
- Vegetable oil
- Additional melted butter, for brushing

Directions:

1. Stir the milk, melted butter, pasteurized egg substitute (or whole egg), sugar, yeast, and salt in a medium bowl to combine. Stir in the flour just until the mixture makes a soft dough.

2. Lightly flour a clean, dry work surface. Turn the dough out onto the work surface. Knead the dough for 5 minutes to develop the gluten.

3. Lightly oil the inside of a clean medium bowl. Gather the dough into a compact ball and set it in the bowl. Turn the dough over so that its surface has oil on it all over. Cover the bowl tightly with plastic wrap and set aside in a warm, draft-free place until the dough has doubled in bulk, about 1½ hours.

4. Punch down the dough, then turn it out onto a clean, dry work surface. Divide it into 5 even balls for a small batch, 6 balls for a medium batch, or 8 balls for a large one.

5. For a small batch, lightly oil the inside of a 6-inch round cake pan and set the balls around its perimeter, separating them as much as possible.

6. For a medium batch, lightly oil the inside of a 7-inch round cake pan and set the balls in it with one ball at its center, separating them as much as possible.

7. For a large batch, lightly oil the inside of an 8-inch round cake pan and set the balls in it with one at the center, separating them as much as possible.

8. Cover with plastic wrap and set aside to rise for 30 minutes.

9. Preheat the air fryer to 350°F .

10. Uncover the pan and brush the rolls with a little melted butter, perhaps ½ teaspoon per roll. When the machine is at temperature, set the cake pan in the basket. Air-fry undisturbed for 14 minutes, or until the rolls have risen and browned.

11. Using kitchen tongs and a nonstick-safe spatula, two hot pads, or silicone baking mitts, transfer the cake pan from the basket to a wire rack. Cool the rolls in the pan for a minute or two. Turn the rolls out onto a wire rack, set them top side up again, and cool for at least another couple of minutes before serving warm.

Crispy Cauliflower Puffs

Servings: 12

Cooking Time: 9 Minutes

Ingredients:

- 1½ cups Riced cauliflower
- 1 cup (about 4 ounces) Shredded Monterey Jack cheese
- ¾ cup Seasoned Italian-style panko bread crumbs (gluten-free, if a concern)
- 2 tablespoons plus 1 teaspoon All-purpose flour or potato starch
- 2 tablespoons plus 1 teaspoon Vegetable oil
- 1 plus 1 large yolk Large egg(s)
- ¾ teaspoon Table salt
- Vegetable oil spray

Directions:

1. Preheat the air fryer to 375°F .

2. Stir the riced cauliflower, cheese, bread crumbs, flour or potato starch, oil, egg(s) and egg yolk (if necessary), and salt in a large bowl to make a thick batter.

3. Using 2 tablespoons of the batter, form a compact ball between your clean, dry palms. Set it aside and continue forming more balls: 7 more for a small batch, 11 more for a medium batch, or 15 more for a large batch.

4. Generously coat the balls on all sides with vegetable oil spray. Set them in the basket with as much air space between them as possible. Air-fry undisturbed for 7 minutes, or until golden brown and crisp. If the machine is at 360°F, you may need to add 2 minutes to the cooking time.

5. Gently pour the contents of the basket onto a wire rack. Cool the puffs for 5 minutes before serving.

Cheesy Texas Toast

Servings: 2

Cooking Time: 4 Minutes

Ingredients:

- ➢ 2 1-inch-thick slice(s) Italian bread (each about 4 inches across)
- ➢ 4 teaspoons Softened butter
- ➢ 2 teaspoons Minced garlic
- ➢ ¼ cup (about ¾ ounce) Finely grated Parmesan cheese

Directions:

1. Preheat the air fryer to 400°F.

2. Spread one side of a slice of bread with 2 teaspoons butter. Sprinkle with 1 teaspoon minced garlic, followed by 2 tablespoons grated cheese. Repeat this process if you're making one or more additional toasts.

3. When the machine is at temperature, put the bread slice(s) cheese side up in the basket (with as much air space between them as possible if you're making more than one). Air-fry undisturbed for 4 minutes, or until browned and crunchy.

4. Use a nonstick-safe spatula to transfer the toasts cheese side up to a wire rack. Cool for 5 minutes before serving.

DESSERTS AND SWEETS

Custard

Servings: 4

Cooking Time: 45 Minutes

Ingredients:

- ➢ 2 cups whole milk
- ➢ 2 eggs
- ➢ ¼ cup sugar
- ➢ ⅛ teaspoon salt
- ➢ ¼ teaspoon vanilla
- ➢ cooking spray
- ➢ ⅛ teaspoon nutmeg

Directions:

1. In a blender, process milk, egg, sugar, salt, and vanilla until smooth.
2. Spray a 6 x 6-inch baking pan with nonstick spray and pour the custard into it.
3. Cook at 300°F for 45 minutes. Custard is done when the center sets.
4. Sprinkle top with the nutmeg.
5. Allow custard to cool slightly.
6. Serve it warm, at room temperature, or chilled.

Pear And Almond Biscotti Crumble

Servings: 6

Cooking Time: 65 Minutes

Ingredients:

- 7-inch cake pan or ceramic dish
- 3 pears, peeled, cored and sliced
- ½ cup brown sugar
- ¼ teaspoon ground ginger
- 1 teaspoon ground cinnamon
- ⅛ teaspoon ground nutmeg
- 2 tablespoons cornstarch
- 1¼ cups (4 to 5) almond biscotti, coarsely crushed
- ¼ cup all-purpose flour
- ¼ cup sliced almonds
- ¼ cup butter, melted

Directions:

1. Combine the pears, brown sugar, ginger, cinnamon, nutmeg and cornstarch in a bowl. Toss to combine and then pour the pear mixture into a greased 7-inch cake pan or ceramic dish.

2. Combine the crushed biscotti, flour, almonds and melted butter in a medium bowl. Toss with a fork until the mixture resembles large crumbles. Sprinkle the biscotti crumble over the pears and cover the pan with aluminum foil.

3. Preheat the air fryer to 350°F.

4. Air-fry at 350°F for 60 minutes. Remove the aluminum foil and air-fry for an additional 5 minutes to brown the crumble layer.

5. Serve warm.

White Chocolate Cranberry Blondies

Servings: 6

Cooking Time: 18 Minutes

Ingredients:

➢ ⅓ cup butter

➢ ½ cup sugar

➢ 1 teaspoon vanilla extract

➢ 1 large egg

➢ 1 cup all-purpose flour

➢ ½ teaspoon baking powder

➢ ⅛ teaspoon salt

➢ ¼ cup dried cranberries

➢ ¼ cup white chocolate chips

Directions:

1. Preheat the air fryer to 320°F.

2. In a large bowl, cream the butter with the sugar and vanilla extract. Whisk in the egg and set aside.

3. In a separate bowl, mix the flour with the baking powder and salt. Then gently mix the dry ingredients into the wet. Fold in the cranberries and chocolate chips.

4. Liberally spray an oven-safe 7-inch springform pan with olive oil and pour the batter into the pan.

5. Cook for 17 minutes or until a toothpick inserted in the center comes out clean.

6. Remove and let cool 5 minutes before serving.

Baked Apple

Servings: 6

Cooking Time: 20 Minutes

Ingredients:

- 3 small Honey Crisp or other baking apples
- 3 tablespoons maple syrup
- 3 tablespoons chopped pecans
- 1 tablespoon firm butter, cut into 6 pieces

Directions:

1. Put ½ cup water in the drawer of the air fryer.
2. Wash apples well and dry them.
3. Split apples in half. Remove core and a little of the flesh to make a cavity for the pecans.
4. Place apple halves in air fryer basket, cut side up.
5. Spoon 1½ teaspoons pecans into each cavity.
6. Spoon ½ tablespoon maple syrup over pecans in each apple.
7. Top each apple with ½ teaspoon butter.
8. Cook at 360°F for 20 minutes, until apples are tender.

Sweet Potato Donut Holes

Servings: 18

Cooking Time: 4 Minutes Per Batch

Ingredients:

- 1 cup flour
- ⅓ cup sugar
- ¼ teaspoon baking soda
- 1 teaspoon baking powder
- ⅛ teaspoon salt
- ½ cup cooked mashed purple sweet potatoes
- 1 egg, beaten
- 2 tablespoons butter, melted
- 1 teaspoon pure vanilla extract
- oil for misting or cooking spray

Directions:

1. Preheat air fryer to 390°F.
2. In a large bowl, stir together the flour, sugar, baking soda, baking powder, and salt.
3. In a separate bowl, combine the potatoes, egg, butter, and vanilla and mix well.
4. Add potato mixture to dry ingredients and stir into a soft dough.
5. Shape dough into 1½-inch balls. Mist lightly with oil or cooking spray.
6. Place 9 donut holes in air fryer basket, leaving a little space in between. Cook for 4 minutes, until done in center and lightly browned outside.
7. Repeat step 6 to cook remaining donut holes.

Brownies After Dark

Servings: 4

Cooking Time: 13 Minutes

Ingredients:

- 1 egg
- ½ cup granulated sugar
- ¼ teaspoon salt
- ½ teaspoon vanilla
- ¼ cup butter, melted
- ¼ cup flour, plus 2 tablespoons
- ¼ cup cocoa
- cooking spray
- Optional
- vanilla ice cream
- caramel sauce
- whipped cream

Directions:

1. Beat together egg, sugar, salt, and vanilla until light.
2. Add melted butter and mix well.
3. Stir in flour and cocoa.
4. Spray 6 x 6-inch baking pan lightly with cooking spray.
5. Spread batter in pan and cook at 330°F for 13 minutes. Cool and cut into 4 large squares or 16 small brownie bites.

Blueberry Crisp

Servings: 6

Cooking Time: 13 Minutes

Ingredients:

- 3 cups Fresh or thawed frozen blueberries
- ⅓ cup Granulated white sugar
- 1 tablespoon Instant tapioca
- ⅓ cup All-purpose flour
- ⅓ cup Rolled oats (not quick-cooking or steel-cut)
- ⅓ cup Chopped walnuts or pecans
- ⅓ cup Packed light brown sugar
- 5 tablespoons plus 1 teaspoon (⅔ stick) Butter, melted and cooled
- ¾ teaspoon Ground cinnamon
- ¼ teaspoon Table salt

Directions:

1. Preheat the air fryer to 400°F.

2. Mix the blueberries, granulated white sugar, and instant tapioca in a 6-inch round cake pan for a small batch, a 7-inch round cake pan for a medium batch, or an 8-inch round cake pan for a large batch.

3. When the machine is at temperature, set the cake pan in the basket and air-fry undisturbed for 5 minutes, or just until the blueberries begin to bubble.

4. Meanwhile, mix the flour, oats, nuts, brown sugar, butter, cinnamon, and salt in a medium bowl until well combined.

5. When the blueberries have begun to bubble, crumble this flour mixture evenly on top. Continue air-frying undisturbed for 8 minutes, or until the topping has browned a bit and the filling is bubbling.

6. Use two hot pads or silicone baking mitts to transfer the cake pan to a wire rack. Cool for at least 10 minutes or to room temperature before serving.

Caramel Apple Crumble

Servings: 6

Cooking Time: 50 Minutes

Ingredients:

- 4 apples, peeled and thinly sliced
- 2 tablespoons sugar
- 1 tablespoon flour
- 1 teaspoon ground cinnamon
- ¼ teaspoon ground allspice
- healthy pinch ground nutmeg
- 10 caramel squares, cut into small pieces
- Crumble Topping:
- ¾ cup rolled oats
- ¼ cup sugar
- ⅓ cup flour
- ¼ teaspoon ground cinnamon
- 6 tablespoons butter, melted

Directions:

1. Preheat the air fryer to 330°F.

2. Combine the apples, sugar, flour, and spices in a large bowl and toss to coat. Add the caramel pieces and mix well. Pour the apple mixture into a 1-quart round baking dish that will fit in your air fryer basket (6-inch diameter).

3. To make the crumble topping, combine the rolled oats, sugar, flour and cinnamon in a small bowl. Add the melted butter and mix well. Top the apples with the crumble mixture. Cover the entire dish with aluminum foil and transfer the dish to the air fryer basket, lowering the dish into the basket using a sling made of aluminum foil (fold a piece of aluminum foil into a strip about 2-inches wide by 24-inches long). Fold the ends of the aluminum foil over the top of the dish before returning the basket to the air fryer.

4. Air-fry at 330°F for 25 minutes. Remove the aluminum foil and continue to air-fry for another 25 minutes. Serve the crumble warm with whipped cream or vanilla ice cream, if desired.

Baked Apple Crisp

Servings: 4

Cooking Time: 23 Minutes

Ingredients:

- ➢ 2 large Granny Smith apples, peeled, cored, and chopped
- ➢ ¼ cup granulated sugar
- ➢ ¼ cup plus 2 teaspoons flour, divided
- ➢ 2 teaspoons milk
- ➢ ¼ teaspoon cinnamon
- ➢ ¼ cup oats
- ➢ ¼ cup brown sugar
- ➢ 2 tablespoons unsalted butter
- ➢ ⅛ teaspoon baking powder
- ➢ ⅛ teaspoon salt

Directions:

1. Preheat the air fryer to 350°F.

2. In a medium bowl, mix the apples, the granulated sugar, 2 teaspoons of the flour, the milk, and the cinnamon.

3. Spray 4 oven-safe ramekins with cooking spray. Divide the filling among the four ramekins.

4. In a small bowl, mix the oats, the brown sugar, the remaining ¼ cup of flour, the butter, the baking powder, and the salt. Use your fingers or a pastry blender to crumble the butter into pea-size pieces. Divide the topping over the top of the apple filling. Cover the apple crisps with foil.

5. Place the covered apple crisps in the air fryer basket and cook for 20 minutes. Uncover and continue cooking for 3 minutes or until the surface is golden and crunchy.

Sea-salted Caramel Cookie Cups

Servings: 12

Cooking Time: 12 Minutes

Ingredients:

- ⅓ cup butter
- ¼ cup brown sugar
- 1 teaspoon vanilla extract
- 1 large egg
- 1 cup all-purpose flour
- ½ cup old-fashioned oats
- ½ teaspoon baking soda
- ¼ teaspoon salt
- ⅓ cup sea-salted caramel chips

Directions:

1. Preheat the air fryer to 300°F.

2. In a large bowl, cream the butter with the brown sugar and vanilla. Whisk in the egg and set aside.

3. In a separate bowl, mix the flour, oats, baking soda, and salt. Then gently mix the dry ingredients into the wet. Fold in the caramel chips.

4. Divide the batter into 12 silicon muffin liners. Place the cookie cups into the air fryer basket and cook for 12 minutes or until a toothpick inserted in the center comes out clean.

5. Remove and let cool 5 minutes before serving.

Chocolate Cake

Servings: 8

Cooking Time: 20 Minutes

Ingredients:

- ½ cup sugar
- ¼ cup flour, plus 3 tablespoons
- 3 tablespoons cocoa
- ½ teaspoon baking powder
- ½ teaspoon baking soda
- ¼ teaspoon salt
- 1 egg
- 2 tablespoons oil
- ½ cup milk
- ½ teaspoon vanilla extract

Directions:

1. Preheat air fryer to 330°F.

2. Grease and flour a 6 x 6-inch baking pan.

3. In a medium bowl, stir together the sugar, flour, cocoa, baking powder, baking soda, and salt.

4. Add all other ingredients and beat with a wire whisk until smooth.

5. Pour batter into prepared pan and bake at 330°F for 20 minutes, until toothpick inserted in center comes out clean or with crumbs clinging to it.

Keto Cheesecake Cups

Servings: 6

Cooking Time: 10 Minutes

Ingredients:

- 8 ounces cream cheese
- ¼ cup plain whole-milk Greek yogurt
- 1 large egg
- 1 teaspoon pure vanilla extract
- 3 tablespoons monk fruit sweetener
- ¼ teaspoon salt
- ½ cup walnuts, roughly chopped

Directions:

1. Preheat the air fryer to 315°F.

2. In a large bowl, use a hand mixer to beat the cream cheese together with the yogurt, egg, vanilla, sweetener, and salt. When combined, fold in the chopped walnuts.

3. Set 6 silicone muffin liners inside an air-fryer-safe pan. Note: This is to allow for an easier time getting the cheesecake bites in and out. If you don't have a pan, you can place them directly in the air fryer basket.

4. Evenly fill the cupcake liners with cheesecake batter.

5. Carefully place the pan into the air fryer basket and cook for about 10 minutes, or until the tops are lightly browned and firm.

6. Carefully remove the pan when done and place in the refrigerator for 3 hours to firm up before serving.

BREAD AND BREAKFAST

Parmesan Garlic Naan

Servings: 6

Cooking Time: 4 Minutes

Ingredients:

➢ 1 cup bread flour

➢ 1 teaspoon baking powder

➢ ⅛ teaspoon salt

➢ 1 teaspoon garlic powder

➢ 2 tablespoon shredded parmesan cheese

➢ 1 cup plain 2% fat Greek yogurt

➢ 1 tablespoon extra-virgin olive oil

Directions:

1. Preheat the air fryer to 400°F.

2. In a medium bowl, mix the flour, baking powder, salt, garlic powder, and cheese. Mix the yogurt into the flour, using your hands to combine if necessary.

3. On a flat surface covered with flour, divide the dough into 6 equal balls and roll each out into a 4-inch-diameter circle.

4. Lightly brush both sides of each naan with olive oil and place one naan at a time into the basket. Cook for 3 to 4 minutes (or until the bread begins to rise and brown on the outside). Remove and repeat for the remaining breads.

5. Serve warm.

Pumpkin Loaf

Servings: 6

Cooking Time: 22 Minutes

Ingredients:

- cooking spray
- 1 large egg
- ½ cup granulated sugar
- ⅓ cup oil
- ½ cup canned pumpkin (not pie filling)
- ½ teaspoon vanilla
- ⅔ cup flour plus 1 tablespoon
- ½ teaspoon baking powder
- ½ teaspoon baking soda
- ½ teaspoon salt
- 1 teaspoon pumpkin pie spice
- ¼ teaspoon cinnamon

Directions:

1. Spray 6 x 6-inch baking dish lightly with cooking spray.
2. Place baking dish in air fryer basket and preheat air fryer to 330°F.
3. In a large bowl, beat eggs and sugar together with a hand mixer.
4. Add oil, pumpkin, and vanilla and mix well.
5. Sift together all dry ingredients. Add to pumpkin mixture and beat well, about 1 minute.
6. Pour batter in baking dish and cook at 330°F for 22 minutes or until toothpick inserted in center of loaf comes out clean.

Soft Pretzels

<table>
<tr><td>Servings: 12</td><td>Cooking Time: 6 Minutes</td></tr>
</table>

Ingredients:

- 2 teaspoons yeast
- 1 cup water, warm
- 1 teaspoon sugar
- 1 teaspoon salt
- 2½ cups all-purpose flour

- 2 tablespoons butter, melted
- 1 cup boiling water
- 1 tablespoon baking soda
- coarse sea salt
- melted butter

Directions:

1. Combine the yeast and water in a small bowl. Combine the sugar, salt and flour in the bowl of a stand mixer. With the mixer running and using the dough hook, drizzle in the yeast mixture and melted butter and knead dough until smooth and elastic – about 10 minutes. Shape into a ball and let the dough rise for 1 hour.

2. Punch the dough down to release any air and decide what size pretzels you want to make.

3. a. To make large pretzels, divide the dough into 12 portions.

4. b. To make medium sized pretzels, divide the dough into 24 portions.

5. c. To make mini pretzel knots, divide the dough into 48 portions.

6. Roll each portion into a skinny rope using both hands on the counter and rolling from the center to the ends of the rope. Spin the rope into a pretzel shape (or tie the rope into a knot) and place the tied pretzels on a parchment lined baking sheet.

7. Preheat the air fryer to 350°F.

8. Combine the boiling water and baking soda in a shallow bowl and whisk to dissolve (this mixture will bubble, but it will settle down). Let the water cool so that you can put your hands in it. Working in batches, dip the pretzels (top side down) into the baking soda-water mixture and let them soak for 30 seconds to a minute. (This step is what gives pretzels their texture and helps them to brown faster.) Then, remove the pretzels carefully and return them (top side up) to the baking sheet. Sprinkle the coarse salt on the top.

9. Air-fry in batches for 3 minutes per side. When the pretzels are finished, brush them generously with the melted butter and enjoy them warm with some spicy mustard.

Strawberry Toast

Servings: 4

Cooking Time: 8 Minutes

Ingredients:

- 4 slices bread, ½-inch thick
- butter-flavored cooking spray
- 1 cup sliced strawberries
- 1 teaspoon sugar

Directions:

1. Spray one side of each bread slice with butter-flavored cooking spray. Lay slices sprayed side down.
2. Divide the strawberries among the bread slices.
3. Sprinkle evenly with the sugar and place in the air fryer basket in a single layer.
4. Cook at 390°F for 8minutes. The bottom should look brown and crisp and the top should look glazed.

Peach Fritters

Servings: 8 Cooking Time: 6 Minutes

Ingredients:

- 1½ cups bread flour
- 1 teaspoon active dry yeast
- ¼ cup sugar
- ¼ teaspoon salt
- ½ cup warm milk
- ½ teaspoon vanilla extract
- 2 egg yolks
- 2 tablespoons melted butter
- 2 cups small diced peaches (fresh or frozen)
- 1 tablespoon butter
- 1 teaspoon ground cinnamon
- 1 to 2 tablespoons sugar
- Glaze
- ¾ cup powdered sugar
- 4 teaspoons milk

Directions:

1. Combine the flour, yeast, sugar and salt in a bowl. Add the milk, vanilla, egg yolks and melted butter and combine until the dough starts to come together. Transfer the dough to a floured surface and knead it by hand for 2 minutes. Shape the dough into a ball, place it in a large oiled bowl, cover with a clean kitchen towel and let the dough rise in a warm place for 1 to 1½ hours, or until the dough has doubled in size.

2. While the dough is rising, melt one tablespoon of butter in a medium saucepan on the stovetop. Add the diced peaches, cinnamon and sugar to taste. Cook the peaches for about 5 minutes, or until they soften. Set the peaches aside to cool.

3. When the dough has risen, transfer it to a floured surface and shape it into a 12-inch circle. Spread the peaches over half of the circle and fold the other half of the dough over the top. With a knife or a board scraper, score the dough by making slits in the dough in a diamond shape. Push the knife straight down into the dough and peaches, rather than slicing through. You should cut through the top layer of dough, but not the bottom. Roll the dough up into a log from one short end to the other. It should be roughly 8 inches long. Some of the peaches will be sticking out of the dough – don't worry, these are supposed to be a little random. Cut the log into 8 equal slices. Place the dough disks on a floured cookie sheet, cover with a clean kitchen towel and let rise in a warm place for 30 minutes.

4. Preheat the air fryer to 370°F.

5. Air-fry 2 or 3 fritters at a time at 370°F, for 3 minutes. Flip them over and continue to air-fry for another 2 to 3 minutes, until they are golden brown.

6. Combine the powdered sugar and milk together in a small bowl. Whisk vigorously until smooth. Allow the fritters to cool for at least 10 minutes and then brush the glaze over both the bottom and top of each one. Serve warm or at room temperature.

Chocolate Chip Banana Muffins

Servings: 12

Cooking Time: 14 Minutes

Ingredients:

- 2 medium bananas, mashed
- ¼ cup brown sugar
- 1½ teaspoons vanilla extract
- ⅔ cup milk
- 2 tablespoons butter
- 1 large egg
- 1 cup white whole-wheat flour
- ½ cup old-fashioned oats
- 1 teaspoon baking soda
- ½ teaspoon baking powder
- ⅛ teaspoon sea salt
- ¼ cup mini chocolate chips

Directions:

1. Preheat the air fryer to 330°F.
2. In a large bowl, combine the bananas, brown sugar, vanilla extract, milk, butter, and egg; set aside.
3. In a separate bowl, combine the flour, oats, baking soda, baking powder, and salt.
4. Slowly add the dry ingredients into the wet ingredients, folding in the flour mixture ⅓ cup at a time.
5. Mix in the chocolate chips and set aside.
6. Using silicone muffin liners, fill 6 muffin liners two-thirds full. Carefully place the muffin liners in the air fryer basket and bake for 20 minutes (or until the tops are browned and a toothpick inserted in the center comes out clean). Carefully remove the muffins from the basket and repeat with the remaining batter.
7. Serve warm.

Egg Muffins

Servings: 4

Cooking Time: 11 Minutes

Ingredients:

- 4 eggs
- salt and pepper
- olive oil
- 4 English muffins, split
- 1 cup shredded Colby Jack cheese
- 4 slices ham or Canadian bacon

Directions:

1. Preheat air fryer to 390°F.

2. Beat together eggs and add salt and pepper to taste. Spray air fryer baking pan lightly with oil and add eggs. Cook for 2minutes, stir, and continue cooking for 4minutes, stirring every minute, until eggs are scrambled to your preference. Remove pan from air fryer.

3. Place bottom halves of English muffins in air fryer basket. Take half of the shredded cheese and divide it among the muffins. Top each with a slice of ham and one-quarter of the eggs. Sprinkle remaining cheese on top of the eggs. Use a fork to press the cheese into the egg a little so it doesn't slip off before it melts.

4. Cook at 360°F for 1 minute. Add English muffin tops and cook for 4minutes to heat through and toast the muffins.

Pepperoni Pizza Bread

Servings: 4

Cooking Time: 15 Minutes

Ingredients:

- 7-inch round bread boule
- 2 cups grated mozzarella cheese
- 1 tablespoon dried oregano
- 1 cup pizza sauce
- 1 cup mini pepperoni or pepperoni slices, cut in quarters
- Pizza sauce for dipping (optional)

Directions:

1. Make 7 to 8 deep slices across the bread boule, leaving 1 inch of bread uncut at the bottom of every slice before you reach the cutting board. The slices should go about three quarters of the way through the boule and be about 2 inches apart from each other. Turn the bread boule 90 degrees and make 7 to 8 similar slices perpendicular to the first slices to form squares in the bread. Again, make sure you don't cut all the way through the bread.

2. Combine the mozzarella cheese and oregano in a small bowl.

3. Fill the slices in the bread with pizza sauce by gently spreading the bread apart and spooning the sauce in between the squares of bread. Top the sauce with the mozzarella cheese mixture and then the pepperoni. Do your very best to get the cheese and pepperoni in between the slices, rather than on top of the bread. Keep spreading the bread apart and stuffing the ingredients in, but be careful not to tear the bottom of the bread.

4. Preheat the air fryer to 320°F.

5. Transfer the bread boule to the air fryer basket and air-fry for 15 minutes, making sure the top doesn't get too dark. (It will just be the cheese on top that gets dark, so if you've done a good job of tucking the cheese in between the slices, this shouldn't be an issue.)

6. Carefully remove the bread from the basket with a spatula. Transfer it to a serving platter with more sauce to dip into if desired. Serve with a lot of napkins so that people can just pull the bread apart with their hands and enjoy!

Orange Rolls

Servings: 8

Cooking Time: 10 Minutes

Ingredients:

- parchment paper
- 3 ounces low-fat cream cheese
- 1 tablespoon low-fat sour cream or plain yogurt (not Greek yogurt)
- 2 teaspoons sugar
- ¼ teaspoon pure vanilla extract
- ¼ teaspoon orange extract
- 1 can (8 count) organic crescent roll dough
- ¼ cup chopped walnuts
- ¼ cup dried cranberries
- ¼ cup shredded, sweetened coconut
- butter-flavored cooking spray
- Orange Glaze
- ½ cup powdered sugar
- 1 tablespoon orange juice
- ¼ teaspoon orange extract
- dash of salt

Directions:

1. Cut a circular piece of parchment paper slightly smaller than the bottom of your air fryer basket. Set aside.

2. In a small bowl, combine the cream cheese, sour cream or yogurt, sugar, and vanilla and orange extracts. Stir until smooth.

3. Preheat air fryer to 300°F.

4. Separate crescent roll dough into 8 triangles and divide cream cheese mixture among them. Starting at wide end, spread cheese mixture to within 1 inch of point.

5. Sprinkle nuts and cranberries evenly over cheese mixture.

6. Starting at wide end, roll up triangles, then sprinkle with coconut, pressing in lightly to make it stick. Spray tops of rolls with butter-flavored cooking spray.

7. Place parchment paper in air fryer basket, and place 4 rolls on top, spaced evenly.

8. Cook for 10minutes, until rolls are golden brown and cooked through.

9. Repeat steps 7 and 8 to cook remaining 4 rolls. You should be able to use the same piece of parchment paper twice.

10. In a small bowl, stir together ingredients for glaze and drizzle over warm rolls.

Wild Blueberry Lemon Chia Bread

Servings: 6

Cooking Time: 27 Minutes

Ingredients:

- ¼ cup extra-virgin olive oil
- ⅓ cup plus 1 tablespoon cane sugar
- 1 large egg
- 3 tablespoons fresh lemon juice
- 1 tablespoon lemon zest
- ⅔ cup milk
- 1 cup all-purpose flour
- ¾ teaspoon baking powder
- ⅛ teaspoon salt
- 2 tablespoons chia seeds
- 1 cup frozen wild blueberries
- ⅓ cup powdered sugar
- 2 teaspoons milk

Directions:

1. Preheat the air fryer to 310°F.
2. In a medium bowl, mix the olive oil with the sugar. Whisk in the egg, lemon juice, lemon zest, and milk; set aside.
3. In a small bowl, combine the all-purpose flour, baking powder, and salt.
4. Slowly mix the dry ingredients into the wet ingredients. Stir in the chia seeds and wild blueberries.
5. Liberally spray a 7-inch springform pan with olive-oil spray. Pour the batter into the pan and place the pan in the air fryer. Bake for 25 to 27 minutes, or until a toothpick inserted in the center comes out clean.
6. Remove and let cool on a wire rack for 10 minutes prior to removing from the pan.
7. Meanwhile, in a small bowl, mix the powdered sugar with the milk to create the glaze.
8. Slice and serve with a drizzle of the powdered sugar glaze.

Pancake Muffins

Servings: 4

Cooking Time: 8 Minutes

Ingredients:

- ➢ 1 cup flour
- ➢ 2 tablespoons sugar (optional)
- ➢ ½ teaspoon baking soda
- ➢ 1 teaspoon baking powder
- ➢ ¼ teaspoon salt
- ➢ 1 egg, beaten
- ➢ 1 cup buttermilk
- ➢ 2 tablespoons melted butter
- ➢ 1 teaspoon pure vanilla extract
- ➢ 24 foil muffin cups
- ➢ cooking spray
- ➢ Suggested Fillings
- ➢ 1 teaspoon of jelly or fruit preserves
- ➢ 1 tablespoon or less fresh blueberries; chopped fresh strawberries; chopped frozen cherries; dark chocolate chips; chopped walnuts, pecans, or other nuts; cooked, crumbled bacon or sausage

Directions:

1. In a large bowl, stir together flour, optional sugar, baking soda, baking powder, and salt.
2. In a small bowl, combine egg, buttermilk, butter, and vanilla. Mix well.
3. Pour egg mixture into dry ingredients and stir to mix well but don't overbeat.
4. Double up the muffin cups and remove the paper liners from the top cups. Spray the foil cups lightly with cooking spray.
5. Place 6 sets of muffin cups in air fryer basket. Pour just enough batter into each cup to cover the bottom. Sprinkle with desired filling. Pour in more batter to cover the filling and fill the cups about ¾ full.
6. Cook at 330°F for 8minutes.
7. Repeat steps 5 and 6 for the remaining 6 pancake muffins.

Fried Pb&j

Servings: 4

Cooking Time: 8 Minutes

Ingredients:

- ½ cup cornflakes, crushed
- ¼ cup shredded coconut
- 8 slices oat nut bread or any whole-grain, oversize bread
- 6 tablespoons peanut butter
- 2 medium bananas, cut into ½-inch-thick slices
- 6 tablespoons pineapple preserves
- 1 egg, beaten
- oil for misting or cooking spray

Directions:

1. Preheat air fryer to 360°F.

2. In a shallow dish, mix together the cornflake crumbs and coconut.

3. For each sandwich, spread one bread slice with 1½ tablespoons of peanut butter. Top with banana slices. Spread another bread slice with 1½ tablespoons of preserves. Combine to make a sandwich.

4. Using a pastry brush, brush top of sandwich lightly with beaten egg. Sprinkle with about 1½ tablespoons of crumb coating, pressing it in to make it stick. Spray with oil.

5. Turn sandwich over and repeat to coat and spray the other side.

6. Cooking 2 at a time, place sandwiches in air fryer basket and cook for 6 to 7minutes or until coating is golden brown and crispy. If sandwich doesn't brown enough, spray with a little more oil and cook at 390°F for another minute.

7. Cut cooked sandwiches in half and serve warm.

VEGETARIANS RECIPES

Roasted Vegetable Stromboli

Servings: 2   Cooking Time: 29 Minutes

Ingredients:

- ½ onion, thinly sliced
- ½ red pepper, julienned
- ½ yellow pepper, julienned
- olive oil
- 1 small zucchini, thinly sliced
- 1 cup thinly sliced mushrooms
- 1½ cups chopped broccoli
- 1 teaspoon Italian seasoning
- salt and freshly ground black pepper
- ½ recipe of Blue Jean Chef Pizza dough (page 231) OR 1 (14-ounce) tube refrigerated pizza dough
- 2 cups grated mozzarella cheese
- ¼ cup grated Parmesan cheese
- ½ cup sliced black olives, optional
- dried oregano
- pizza or marinara sauce

Directions:

1. Preheat the air fryer to 400°F.

2. Toss the onions and peppers with a little olive oil and air-fry the vegetables for 7 minutes, shaking the basket once or twice while the vegetables cook. Add the zucchini, mushrooms, broccoli and Italian seasoning to the basket. Add a little more olive oil and season with salt and freshly ground black pepper. Air-fry for an additional 7 minutes, shaking the basket halfway through. Let the vegetables cool slightly while you roll out the pizza dough.

3. On a lightly floured surface, roll or press the pizza dough out into a 13-inch by 11-inch rectangle, with the long side closest to you. Sprinkle half of the mozzarella and Parmesan cheeses over the dough leaving an empty 1-inch border from the edge farthest away from you. Spoon the roasted vegetables over the cheese, sprinkle the olives over everything and top with the remaining cheese.

4. Start rolling the stromboli away from you and toward the empty border. Make sure the filling stays tightly tucked inside the roll. Finally, tuck the ends of the dough in and pinch the seam shut. Place the seam side down and shape the stromboli into a U-shape to fit into the air fryer basket. Cut 4 small slits with the tip of a sharp knife evenly in the top of the dough, lightly brush the stromboli with a little oil and sprinkle with some dried oregano.

5. Preheat the air fryer to 360°F.

6. Spray or brush the air fryer basket with oil and transfer the U-shaped stromboli to the air fryer basket. Air-fry for 15 minutes, flipping the stromboli over after the first 10 minutes. (Use a plate to invert the Stromboli out of the air fryer basket and then slide it back into the basket off the plate.)

7. To remove, carefully flip the stromboli over onto a cutting board. Let it rest for a couple of minutes before serving. Cut it into 2-inch slices and serve with pizza or marinara sauce.

Spicy Sesame Tempeh Slaw With Peanut Dressing

Servings: 2

Cooking Time: 8 Minutes

Ingredients:

- 2 cups hot water
- 1 teaspoon salt
- 8 ounces tempeh, sliced into 1-inch-long pieces
- 2 tablespoons low-sodium soy sauce
- 2 tablespoons rice vinegar
- 1 tablespoon filtered water
- 2 teaspoons sesame oil
- ½ teaspoon fresh ginger
- 1 clove garlic, minced
- ¼ teaspoon black pepper
- ½ jalapeño, sliced
- 4 cups cabbage slaw
- 4 tablespoons Peanut Dressing (see the following recipe)
- 2 tablespoons fresh chopped cilantro
- 2 tablespoons chopped peanuts

Directions:

1. Mix the hot water with the salt and pour over the tempeh in a glass bowl. Stir and cover with a towel for 10 minutes.

2. Discard the water and leave the tempeh in the bowl.

3. In a medium bowl, mix the soy sauce, rice vinegar, filtered water, sesame oil, ginger, garlic, pepper, and jalapeño. Pour over the tempeh and cover with a towel. Place in the refrigerator to marinate for at least 2 hours.

4. Preheat the air fryer to 370°F. Remove the tempeh from the bowl and discard the remaining marinade.

5. Liberally spray the metal trivet that goes into the air fryer basket and place the tempeh on top of the trivet.

6. Cook for 4 minutes, flip, and cook another 4 minutes.

7. In a large bowl, mix the cabbage slaw with the Peanut Dressing and toss in the cilantro and chopped peanuts.

8. Portion onto 4 plates and place the cooked tempeh on top when cooking completes. Serve immediately.

Spicy Vegetable And Tofu Shake Fry

Servings: 4   Cooking Time: 17 Minutes

Ingredients:

- 4 teaspoons canola oil, divided
- 2 tablespoons rice wine vinegar
- 1 tablespoon sriracha chili sauce
- ¼ cup soy sauce*
- ½ teaspoon toasted sesame oil
- 1 teaspoon minced garlic
- 1 tablespoon minced fresh ginger
- 8 ounces extra firm tofu
- ½ cup vegetable stock or water
- 1 tablespoon honey
- 1 tablespoon cornstarch
- ½ red onion, chopped
- 1 red or yellow bell pepper, chopped
- 1 cup green beans, cut into 2-inch lengths
- 4 ounces mushrooms, sliced
- 2 scallions, sliced
- 2 tablespoons fresh cilantro leaves
- 2 teaspoons toasted sesame seeds

Directions:

1. Combine 1 tablespoon of the oil, vinegar, sriracha sauce, soy sauce, sesame oil, garlic and ginger in a small bowl. Cut the tofu into bite-sized cubes and toss the tofu in with the marinade while you prepare the other vegetables. When you are ready to start cooking, remove the tofu from the marinade and set it aside. Add the water, honey and cornstarch to the marinade and bring to a simmer on the stovetop, just until the sauce thickens. Set the sauce aside.

2. Preheat the air fryer to 400°F.

3. Toss the onion, pepper, green beans and mushrooms in a bowl with a little canola oil and season with salt. Air-fry at 400°F for 11 minutes, shaking the basket and tossing the vegetables every few minutes. When the vegetables are cooked to your preferred doneness, remove them from the air fryer and set aside.

4. Add the tofu to the air fryer basket and air-fry at 400°F for 6 minutes, shaking the basket a few times during the cooking process. Add the vegetables back to the basket and air-fry for another minute. Transfer the vegetables and tofu to a large bowl, add the scallions and cilantro leaves and toss with the sauce. Serve over rice with sesame seeds sprinkled on top.

Roasted Vegetable Thai Green Curry

Servings: 4

Cooking Time: 16 Minutes

Ingredients:

- 1 (13-ounce) can coconut milk
- 3 tablespoons green curry paste
- 1 tablespoon soy sauce*
- 1 tablespoon rice wine vinegar
- 1 teaspoon sugar
- 1 teaspoon minced fresh ginger
- ½ onion, chopped
- 3 carrots, sliced
- 1 red bell pepper, chopped
- olive oil
- 10 stalks of asparagus, cut into 2-inch pieces
- 3 cups broccoli florets
- basmati rice for serving
- fresh cilantro
- crushed red pepper flakes (optional)

Directions:

1. Combine the coconut milk, green curry paste, soy sauce, rice wine vinegar, sugar and ginger in a medium saucepan and bring to a boil on the stovetop. Reduce the heat and simmer for 20 minutes while you cook the vegetables. Set aside.

2. Preheat the air fryer to 400°F.

3. Toss the onion, carrots, and red pepper together with a little olive oil and transfer the vegetables to the air fryer basket. Air-fry at 400°F for 10 minutes, shaking the basket a few times during the cooking process. Add the asparagus and broccoli florets and air-fry for an additional 6 minutes, again shaking the basket for even cooking.

4. When the vegetables are cooked to your liking, toss them with the green curry sauce and serve in bowls over basmati rice. Garnish with fresh chopped cilantro and crushed red pepper flakes.

Cauliflower Steaks Gratin

Servings: 2

Cooking Time: 13 Minutes

Ingredients:

➢ 1 head cauliflower

➢ 1 tablespoon olive oil

➢ salt and freshly ground black pepper

➢ ½ teaspoon chopped fresh thyme leaves

➢ 3 tablespoons grated Parmigiano-Reggiano cheese

➢ 2 tablespoons panko breadcrumbs

Directions:

1. Preheat the air-fryer to 370°F.

2. Cut two steaks out of the center of the cauliflower. To do this, cut the cauliflower in half and then cut one slice about 1-inch thick off each half. The rest of the cauliflower will fall apart into florets, which you can roast on their own or save for another meal.

3. Brush both sides of the cauliflower steaks with olive oil and season with salt, freshly ground black pepper and fresh thyme. Place the cauliflower steaks into the air fryer basket and air-fry for 6 minutes. Turn the steaks over and air-fry for another 4 minutes. Combine the Parmesan cheese and panko breadcrumbs and sprinkle the mixture over the tops of both steaks and air-fry for another 3 minutes until the cheese has melted and the breadcrumbs have browned. Serve this with some sautéed bitter greens and air-fried blistered tomatoes.

Cheese Ravioli

Servings: 4

Cooking Time: 9 Minutes

Ingredients:

- 1 egg
- ¼ cup milk
- 1 cup breadcrumbs
- 2 teaspoons Italian seasoning
- ⅛ teaspoon ground rosemary
- ¼ teaspoon basil
- ¼ teaspoon parsley
- 9-ounce package uncooked cheese ravioli
- ¼ cup flour
- oil for misting or cooking spray

Directions:

1. Preheat air fryer to 390°F.
2. In a medium bowl, beat together egg and milk.
3. In a large plastic bag, mix together the breadcrumbs, Italian seasoning, rosemary, basil, and parsley.
4. Place all the ravioli and the flour in a bag or a bowl with a lid and shake to coat.
5. Working with a handful at a time, drop floured ravioli into egg wash. Remove ravioli, letting excess drip off, and place in bag with breadcrumbs.
6. When all ravioli are in the breadcrumbs' bag, shake well to coat all pieces.
7. Dump enough ravioli into air fryer basket to form one layer. Mist with oil or cooking spray. Dump the remaining ravioli on top of the first layer and mist with oil.
8. Cook for 5minutes. Shake well and spray with oil. Break apart any ravioli stuck together and spray any spots you missed the first time.
9. Cook 4 minutes longer, until ravioli puff up and are crispy golden brown.

Corn And Pepper Jack Chile Rellenos With Roasted Tomato Sauce

Servings: 3   Cooking Time: 30 Minutes

Ingredients:

- 3 Poblano peppers
- 1 cup all-purpose flour*
- salt and freshly ground black pepper
- 2 eggs, lightly beaten
- 1 cup plain breadcrumbs*
- olive oil, in a spray bottle
- Sauce
- 2 cups cherry tomatoes
- 1 Jalapeño pepper, halved and seeded
- 1 clove garlic

- ¼ red onion, broken into large pieces
- 1 tablespoon olive oil
- salt, to taste
- 2 tablespoons chopped fresh cilantro
- Filling
- olive oil
- ¼ red onion, finely chopped
- 1 teaspoon minced garlic
- 1 cup corn kernels, fresh or frozen
- 2 cups grated pepper jack cheese

Directions:

1. Start by roasting the peppers. Preheat the air fryer to 400°F. Place the peppers into the air fryer basket and air-fry at 400°F for 10 minutes, turning them over halfway through the cooking time. Remove the peppers from the basket and cover loosely with foil.

2. While the peppers are cooling, make the roasted tomato sauce. Place all sauce Ingredients except for the cilantro into the air fryer basket and air-fry at 400°F for 10 minutes, shaking the basket once or twice. When the sauce Ingredients have finished air-frying, transfer everything to a blender or food processor and blend or process to a smooth sauce, adding a little warm water to get the desired consistency. Season to taste with salt, add the cilantro and set aside.

3. While the sauce Ingredients are cooking in the air fryer, make the filling. Heat a skillet on the stovetop over medium heat. Add the olive oil and sauté the red onion and garlic for 4 to 5 minutes. Transfer the onion and garlic to a bowl, stir in the corn and cheese, and set aside.

4. Set up a dredging station with three shallow dishes. Place the flour, seasoned with salt and pepper, in the first shallow dish. Place the eggs in the second dish, and fill the third shallow dish with the breadcrumbs. When the peppers have cooled, carefully slice into one side of the pepper to create an opening. Pull the seeds out of the peppers and peel away the skins, trying not to tear the pepper. Fill each pepper with some of the corn and cheese filling and close the pepper up again by folding one side of the opening over the other. Carefully roll each pepper in the seasoned flour, then into the egg and finally into the breadcrumbs to coat on all sides, trying not to let the pepper fall open. Spray the peppers on all sides with a little olive oil.

5. Air-fry two peppers at a time at 350°F for 6 minutes. Turn the peppers over and air-fry for another 4 minutes. Serve the peppers warm on a bed of the roasted tomato sauce.

Spinach And Cheese Calzone

Servings: 2

Cooking Time: 10 Minutes

Ingredients:

- ⅔ cup frozen chopped spinach, thawed
- 1 cup grated mozzarella cheese
- 1 cup ricotta cheese
- ½ teaspoon Italian seasoning
- ½ teaspoon salt
- freshly ground black pepper
- 1 store-bought or homemade pizza dough* (about 12 to 16 ounces)
- 2 tablespoons olive oil
- pizza or marinara sauce (optional)

Directions:

1. Drain and squeeze all the water out of the thawed spinach and set it aside. Mix the mozzarella cheese, ricotta cheese, Italian seasoning, salt and freshly ground black pepper together in a bowl. Stir in the chopped spinach.

2. Divide the dough in half. With floured hands or on a floured surface, stretch or roll one half of the dough into a 10-inch circle. Spread half of the cheese and spinach mixture on half of the dough, leaving about one inch of dough empty around the edge.

3. Fold the other half of the dough over the cheese mixture, almost to the edge of the bottom dough to form a half moon. Fold the bottom edge of dough up over the top edge and crimp the dough around the edges in order to make the crust and seal the calzone. Brush the dough with olive oil. Repeat with the second half of dough to make the second calzone.

4. Preheat the air fryer to 360°F.

5. Brush or spray the air fryer basket with olive oil. Air-fry the calzones one at a time for 10 minutes, flipping the calzone over half way through. Serve with warm pizza or marinara sauce if desired.

Egg Rolls

Servings: 4

Cooking Time: 8 Minutes

Ingredients:

➢ 1 clove garlic, minced

➢ 1 teaspoon sesame oil

➢ 1 teaspoon olive oil

➢ ½ cup chopped celery

➢ ½ cup grated carrots

➢ 2 green onions, chopped

➢ 2 ounces mushrooms, chopped

➢ 2 cups shredded Napa cabbage

➢ 1 teaspoon low-sodium soy sauce

➢ 1 teaspoon cornstarch

➢ salt

➢ 1 egg

➢ 1 tablespoon water

➢ 4 egg roll wraps

➢ olive oil for misting or cooking spray

Directions:

1. In a large skillet, sauté garlic in sesame and olive oils over medium heat for 1 minute.

2. Add celery, carrots, onions, and mushrooms to skillet. Cook 1 minute, stirring.

3. Stir in cabbage, cover, and cook for 1 minute or just until cabbage slightly wilts.

4. In a small bowl, mix soy sauce and cornstarch. Stir into vegetables to thicken. Remove from heat. Salt to taste if needed.

5. Beat together egg and water in a small bowl.

6. Divide filling into 4 portions and roll up in egg roll wraps. Brush all over with egg wash to seal.

7. Mist egg rolls very lightly with olive oil or cooking spray and place in air fryer basket.

8. Cook at 390°F for 4minutes. Turn over and cook 4 more minutes, until golden brown and crispy.

Rigatoni With Roasted Onions, Fennel, Spinach And Lemon Pepper Ricotta

Servings: 2

Cooking Time: 13 Minutes

Ingredients:

- 1 red onion, rough chopped into large chunks
- 2 teaspoons olive oil, divided
- 1 bulb fennel, sliced ¼-inch thick
- ¾ cup ricotta cheese
- 1½ teaspoons finely chopped lemon zest, plus more for garnish
- 1 teaspoon lemon juice
- salt and freshly ground black pepper
- 8 ounces (½ pound) dried rigatoni pasta
- 3 cups baby spinach leaves

Directions:

1. Bring a large stockpot of salted water to a boil on the stovetop and Preheat the air fryer to 400°F.

2. While the water is coming to a boil, toss the chopped onion in 1 teaspoon of olive oil and transfer to the air fryer basket. Air-fry at 400°F for 5 minutes. Toss the sliced fennel with 1 teaspoon of olive oil and add this to the air fryer basket with the onions. Continue to air-fry at 400°F for 8 minutes, shaking the basket a few times during the cooking process.

3. Combine the ricotta cheese, lemon zest and juice, ¼ teaspoon of salt and freshly ground black pepper in a bowl and stir until smooth.

4. Add the dried rigatoni to the boiling water and cook according to the package directions. When the pasta is cooked al dente, reserve one cup of the pasta water and drain the pasta into a colander.

5. Place the spinach in a serving bowl and immediately transfer the hot pasta to the bowl, wilting the spinach. Add the roasted onions and fennel and toss together. Add a little pasta water to the dish if it needs moistening. Then, dollop the lemon pepper ricotta cheese on top and nestle it into the hot pasta. Garnish with more lemon zest if desired.

Eggplant Parmesan

Servings: 4

Cooking Time: 8 Minutes Per Batch

Ingredients:

- 1 medium eggplant, 6–8 inches long
- salt
- 1 large egg
- 1 tablespoon water
- ⅔ cup panko breadcrumbs
- ⅓ cup grated Parmesan cheese, plus more for serving
- 1 tablespoon Italian seasoning
- ¾ teaspoon oregano
- oil for misting or cooking spray
- 1 24-ounce jar marinara sauce
- 8 ounces spaghetti, cooked
- pepper

Directions:

1. Preheat air fryer to 390°F.
2. Leaving peel intact, cut eggplant into 8 round slices about ¾-inch thick. Salt to taste.
3. Beat egg and water in a shallow dish.
4. In another shallow dish, combine panko, Parmesan, Italian seasoning, and oregano.
5. Dip eggplant slices in egg wash and then crumbs, pressing lightly to coat.
6. Mist slices with oil or cooking spray.
7. Place 4 eggplant slices in air fryer basket and cook for 8 minutes, until brown and crispy.
8. While eggplant is cooking, heat marinara sauce.
9. Repeat step 7 to cook remaining eggplant slices.
10. To serve, place cooked spaghetti on plates and top with marinara and eggplant slices. At the table, pass extra Parmesan cheese and freshly ground black pepper.

Tacos

Servings: 24

Cooking Time: 8 Minutes Per Batch

Ingredients:

➢ 1 24-count package 4-inch corn tortillas

➢ 1½ cups refried beans (about ¾ of a 15-ounce can)

➢ 4 ounces sharp Cheddar cheese, grated

➢ ½ cup salsa

➢ oil for misting or cooking spray

Directions:

1. Preheat air fryer to 390°F.

2. Wrap refrigerated tortillas in damp paper towels and microwave for 30 to 60 seconds to warm. If necessary, rewarm tortillas as you go to keep them soft enough to fold without breaking.

3. Working with one tortilla at a time, top with 1 tablespoon of beans, 1 tablespoon of grated cheese, and 1 teaspoon of salsa. Fold over and press down very gently on the center. Press edges firmly all around to seal. Spray both sides with oil or cooking spray.

4. Cooking in two batches, place half the tacos in the air fryer basket. To cook 12 at a time, you may need to stand them upright and lean some against the sides of basket. It's okay if they're crowded as long as you leave a little room for air to circulate around them.

5. Cook for 8 minutes or until golden brown and crispy.

6. Repeat steps 4 and 5 to cook remaining tacos.

FISH AND SEAFOOD RECIPES

Sesame-crusted Tuna Steaks

Servings:3

Cooking Time: 10-13 Minutes

Ingredients:

- ½ cup Sesame seeds, preferably a blend of white and black
- 1½ tablespoons Toasted sesame oil
- 3 6-ounce skinless tuna steaks

Directions:

1. Preheat the air fryer to 400°F.

2. Pour the sesame seeds on a dinner plate. Use ½ tablespoon of the sesame oil as a rub on both sides and the edges of a tuna steak. Set it in the sesame seeds, then turn it several times, pressing gently, to create an even coating of the seeds, including around the steak's edge. Set aside and continue coating the remaining steak(s).

3. When the machine is at temperature, set the steaks in the basket with as much air space between them as possible. Air-fry undisturbed for 10 minutes for medium-rare (not USDA-approved), or 12 to 13 minutes for cooked through (USDA-approved).

4. Use a nonstick-safe spatula to transfer the steaks to serving plates. Serve hot.

Perfect Soft-shelled Crabs

Servings:2

Cooking Time: 12 Minutes

Ingredients:

- ½ cup All-purpose flour
- 1 tablespoon Old Bay seasoning
- 1 Large egg(s), well beaten
- 1 cup (about 3 ounces) Ground oyster crackers
- 2 2½-ounce cleaned soft-shelled crab(s), about 4 inches across
- Vegetable oil spray

Directions:

1. Preheat the air fryer to 375°F (or 380°F or 390°F, if one of these is the closest setting).

2. Set up and fill three shallow soup plates or small pie plates on your counter: one for the flour, whisked with the Old Bay until well combined; one for the beaten egg(s); and one for the cracker crumbs.

3. Set a soft-shelled crab in the flour mixture and turn to coat evenly and well on all sides, even inside the legs. Dip the crab into the egg(s) and coat well, turning at least once, again getting some of the egg between the legs. Let any excess egg slip back into the rest, then set the crab in the cracker crumbs. Turn several times, pressing very gently to get the crab evenly coated with crumbs, even between the legs. Generously coat the crab on all sides with vegetable oil spray. Set it aside if you're making more than one and coat these in the same way.

4. Set the crab(s) in the basket with as much air space between them as possible. They may overlap slightly, particularly at the ends of their legs, depending on the basket's size. Air-fry undisturbed for 12 minutes, or until very crisp and golden brown. If the machine is at 390°F, the crabs may be done in only 10 minutes.

5. Use kitchen tongs to gently transfer the crab(s) to a wire rack. Cool for a couple of minutes before serving.

Crunchy And Buttery Cod With Ritz® Cracker Crust

Servings: 2

Cooking Time: 10 Minutes

Ingredients:

- 4 tablespoons butter, melted
- 8 to 10 RITZ® crackers, crushed into crumbs
- 2 (6-ounce) cod fillets
- salt and freshly ground black pepper
- 1 lemon

Directions:

1. Preheat the air fryer to 380°F.

2. Melt the butter in a small saucepan on the stovetop or in a microwavable dish in the microwave, and then transfer the butter to a shallow dish. Place the crushed RITZ® crackers into a second shallow dish.

3. Season the fish fillets with salt and freshly ground black pepper. Dip them into the butter and then coat both sides with the RITZ® crackers.

4. Place the fish into the air fryer basket and air-fry at 380°F for 10 minutes, flipping the fish over halfway through the cooking time.

5. Serve with a wedge of lemon to squeeze over the top.

Shrimp, Chorizo And Fingerling Potatoes

Servings: 4

Cooking Time: 16 Minutes

Ingredients:

- ½ red onion, chopped into 1-inch chunks
- 8 fingerling potatoes, sliced into 1-inch slices or halved lengthwise
- 1 teaspoon olive oil
- salt and freshly ground black pepper
- 8 ounces raw chorizo sausage, sliced into 1-inch chunks
- 16 raw large shrimp, peeled, deveined and tails removed
- 1 lime
- ¼ cup chopped fresh cilantro
- chopped orange zest (optional)

Directions:

1. Preheat the air fryer to 380°F.

2. Combine the red onion and potato chunks in a bowl and toss with the olive oil, salt and freshly ground black pepper.

3. Transfer the vegetables to the air fryer basket and air-fry for 6 minutes, shaking the basket a few times during the cooking process.

4. Add the chorizo chunks and continue to air-fry for another 5 minutes.

5. Add the shrimp, season with salt and continue to air-fry, shaking the basket every once in a while, for another 5 minutes.

6. Transfer the tossed shrimp, chorizo and potato to a bowl and squeeze some lime juice over the top to taste. Toss in the fresh cilantro, orange zest and a drizzle of olive oil, and season again to taste.

7. Serve with a fresh green salad.

Blackened Red Snapper

Servings: 4

Cooking Time: 8 Minutes

Ingredients:

- 1½ teaspoons black pepper
- ¼ teaspoon thyme
- ¼ teaspoon garlic powder
- ⅛ teaspoon cayenne pepper
- 1 teaspoon olive oil
- 4 4-ounce red snapper fillet portions, skin on
- 4 thin slices lemon
- cooking spray

Directions:

1. Mix the spices and oil together to make a paste. Rub into both sides of the fish.
2. Spray air fryer basket with nonstick cooking spray and lay snapper steaks in basket, skin-side down.
3. Place a lemon slice on each piece of fish.
4. Cook at 390°F for 8 minutes. The fish will not flake when done, but it should be white through the center.

Spicy Fish Street Tacos With Sriracha Slaw

Servings: 2

Cooking Time: 5 Minutes

Ingredients:

- Sriracha Slaw:
- ½ cup mayonnaise
- 2 tablespoons rice vinegar
- 1 teaspoon sugar
- 2 tablespoons sriracha chili sauce
- 5 cups shredded green cabbage
- ¼ cup shredded carrots
- 2 scallions, chopped
- salt and freshly ground black pepper
- Tacos:
- ½ cup flour
- 1 teaspoon chili powder
- ½ teaspoon ground cumin
- 1 teaspoon salt
- freshly ground black pepper
- ½ teaspoon baking powder
- 1 egg, beaten
- ¼ cup milk
- 1 cup breadcrumbs
- 1 pound mahi-mahi or snapper fillets
- 1 tablespoon canola or vegetable oil
- 6 (6-inch) flour tortillas
- 1 lime, cut into wedges

Directions:

1. Start by making the sriracha slaw. Combine the mayonnaise, rice vinegar, sugar, and sriracha sauce in a large bowl. Mix well and add the green cabbage, carrots, and scallions. Toss until all the vegetables are coated with the dressing and season with salt and pepper. Refrigerate the slaw until you are ready to serve the tacos.

2. Combine the flour, chili powder, cumin, salt, pepper and baking powder in a bowl. Add the egg and milk and mix until the batter is smooth. Place the breadcrumbs in shallow dish.

3. Cut the fish fillets into 1-inch wide sticks, approximately 4-inches long. You should have about 12 fish sticks total. Dip the fish sticks into the batter, coating all sides. Let the excess batter drip off the fish and then roll them in the breadcrumbs, patting the crumbs onto all sides of the fish sticks. Set the coated fish on a plate or baking sheet until all the fish has been coated.

4. Preheat the air fryer to 400°F.

5. Spray the coated fish sticks with oil on all sides. Spray or brush the inside of the air fryer basket with oil and transfer the fish to the basket. Place as many sticks as you can in one layer, leaving a little room around each stick. Place any remaining sticks on top, perpendicular to the first layer.

6. Air-fry the fish for 3 minutes. Turn the fish sticks over and air-fry for an additional 2 minutes.

7. While the fish is air-frying, warm the tortilla shells either in a 350°F oven wrapped in foil or in a skillet with a little oil over medium-high heat for a couple minutes. Fold the tortillas in half and keep them warm until the remaining tortillas and fish are ready.

8. To assemble the tacos, place two pieces of the fish in each tortilla shell and top with the sriracha slaw. Squeeze the lime wedge over top and dig in.

Crab Cakes

Servings: 2   Cooking Time: 10 Minutes

Ingredients:

- 1 teaspoon butter
- ⅓ cup finely diced onion
- ⅓ cup finely diced celery
- ¼ cup mayonnaise
- 1 teaspoon Dijon mustard
- 1 egg
- pinch ground cayenne pepper
- 1 teaspoon salt
- freshly ground black pepper
- 16 ounces lump crabmeat
- ½ cup + 2 tablespoons panko breadcrumbs, divided

Directions:

1. Melt the butter in a skillet over medium heat. Sauté the onion and celery until it starts to soften, but not brown – about 4 minutes. Transfer the cooked vegetables to a large bowl. Add the mayonnaise, Dijon mustard, egg, cayenne pepper, salt and freshly ground black pepper to the bowl. Gently fold in the lump crabmeat and 2 tablespoons of panko breadcrumbs. Stir carefully so you don't break up all the crab pieces.

2. Preheat the air fryer to 400°F.

3. Place the remaining panko breadcrumbs in a shallow dish. Divide the crab mixture into 4 portions and shape each portion into a round patty. Dredge the crab patties in the breadcrumbs, coating both sides as well as the edges with the crumbs.

4. Air-fry the crab cakes for 5 minutes. Using a flat spatula, gently turn the cakes over and air-fry for another 5 minutes. Serve the crab cakes with tartar sauce or cocktail sauce, or dress it up with the suggestion below.

Italian Tuna Roast

Servings: 8

Cooking Time: 21 Minutes

Ingredients:

- cooking spray
- 1 tablespoon Italian seasoning
- ⅛ teaspoon ground black pepper
- 1 tablespoon extra-light olive oil
- 1 teaspoon lemon juice
- 1 tuna loin (approximately 2 pounds, 3 to 4 inches thick, large enough to fill a 6 x 6-inch baking dish)

Directions:

1. Spray baking dish with cooking spray and place in air fryer basket. Preheat air fryer to 390°F.
2. Mix together the Italian seasoning, pepper, oil, and lemon juice.
3. Using a dull table knife or butter knife, pierce top of tuna about every half inch: Insert knife into top of tuna roast and pierce almost all the way to the bottom.
4. Spoon oil mixture into each of the holes and use the knife to push seasonings into the tuna as deeply as possible.
5. Spread any remaining oil mixture on all outer surfaces of tuna.
6. Place tuna roast in baking dish and cook at 390°F for 20 minutes. Check temperature with a meat thermometer. Cook for an additional 1 minutes or until temperature reaches 145°F.
7. Remove basket from fryer and let tuna sit in basket for 10minutes.

Cajun Flounder Fillets

Servings:2

Cooking Time: 5 Minutes

Ingredients:

- 2 4-ounce skinless flounder fillet(s)
- 2 teaspoons Peanut oil
- 1 teaspoon Purchased or homemade Cajun dried seasoning blend (see the headnote)

Directions:

1. Preheat the air fryer to 400°F.

2. Oil the fillet(s) by drizzling on the peanut oil, then gently rubbing in the oil with your clean, dry fingers. Sprinkle the seasoning blend evenly over both sides of the fillet(s).

3. When the machine is at temperature, set the fillet(s) in the basket. If working with more than one fillet, they should not touch, although they may be quite close together, depending on the basket's size. Air-fry undisturbed for 5 minutes, or until lightly browned and cooked through.

4. Use a nonstick-safe spatula to transfer the fillets to a serving platter or plate(s). Serve at once.

Garlic And Dill Salmon

Servings: 2

Cooking Time: 8 Minutes

Ingredients:

- 12 ounces salmon filets with skin
- 2 tablespoons melted butter
- 1 tablespoon extra-virgin olive oil
- 2 garlic cloves, minced
- 1 tablespoon fresh dill
- ½ teaspoon sea salt
- ½ lemon

Directions:

1. Pat the salmon dry with paper towels.
2. In a small bowl, mix together the melted butter, olive oil, garlic, and dill.
3. Sprinkle the top of the salmon with sea salt. Brush all sides of the salmon with the garlic and dill butter.
4. Preheat the air fryer to 350°F.
5. Place the salmon, skin side down, in the air fryer basket. Cook for 6 to 8 minutes, or until the fish flakes in the center.
6. Remove the salmon and plate on a serving platter. Squeeze fresh lemon over the top of the salmon. Serve immediately.

Crunchy Clam Strips

Servings:3

Cooking Time: 8 Minutes

Ingredients:

- ½ pound Clam strips, drained
- 1 Large egg, well beaten
- ½ cup All-purpose flour
- ½ cup Yellow cornmeal
- 1½ teaspoons Table salt
- 1½ teaspoons Ground black pepper
- Up to ¾ teaspoon Cayenne
- Vegetable oil spray

Directions:

1. Preheat the air fryer to 400°F.

2. Toss the clam strips and beaten egg in a bowl until the clams are well coated.

3. Mix the flour, cornmeal, salt, pepper, and cayenne in a large zip-closed plastic bag until well combined. Using a flatware fork or small kitchen tongs, lift the clam strips one by one out of the egg, letting any excess egg slip back into the rest. Put the strips in the bag with the flour mixture. Once all the strips are in the bag, seal it and shake gently until the strips are well coated.

4. Use kitchen tongs to pick out the clam strips and lay them on a cutting board (leaving any extra flour mixture in the bag to be discarded). Coat the strips on both sides with vegetable oil spray.

5. When the machine is at temperature, spread the clam strips in the basket in one layer. They may touch in places, but try to leave as much air space as possible around them. Air-fry undisturbed for 8 minutes, or until brown and crunchy.

6. Gently dump the contents of the basket onto a serving platter. Cool for just a minute or two before serving hot.

Chicken Spiedies

Servings: 3   Cooking Time: 12 Minutes

Ingredients:

- 1¼ pounds Boneless skinless chicken thighs, trimmed of any fat blobs and cut into 2-inch pieces
- 3 tablespoons Red wine vinegar
- 2 tablespoons Olive oil
- 2 tablespoons Minced fresh mint leaves
- 2 tablespoons Minced fresh parsley leaves
- 2 teaspoons Minced fresh dill fronds
- ¾ teaspoon Fennel seeds
- ¾ teaspoon Table salt
- Up to a ¼ teaspoon Red pepper flakes
- 3 Long soft rolls, such as hero, hoagie, or Italian sub rolls (gluten-free, if a concern), split open lengthwise
- 4½ tablespoons Regular or low-fat mayonnaise (not fat-free; gluten-free, if a concern)
- 1½ tablespoons Distilled white vinegar
- 1½ teaspoons Ground black pepper

Directions:

1. Mix the chicken, vinegar, oil, mint, parsley, dill, fennel seeds, salt, and red pepper flakes in a zip-closed plastic bag. Seal, gently massage the marinade ingredients into the meat, and refrigerate for at least 2 hours or up to 6 hours. (Longer than that and the meat can turn rubbery.)

2. Set the plastic bag out on the counter (to make the contents a little less frigid). Preheat the air fryer to 400°F.

3. When the machine is at temperature, use kitchen tongs to set the chicken thighs in the basket (discard any remaining marinade) and air-fry undisturbed for 6 minutes. Turn the thighs over and continue air-frying undisturbed for 6 minutes more, until well browned, cooked through, and even a little crunchy.

4. Dump the contents of the basket onto a wire rack and cool for 2 or 3 minutes. Divide the chicken evenly between the rolls. Whisk the mayonnaise, vinegar, and black pepper in a small bowl until smooth. Drizzle this sauce over the chicken pieces in the rolls.

Chicken Club Sandwiches

Servings: 3

Cooking Time: 15 Minutes

Ingredients:

- 3 5- to 6-ounce boneless skinless chicken breasts
- 6 Thick-cut bacon strips (gluten-free, if a concern)
- 3 Long soft rolls, such as hero, hoagie, or Italian sub rolls (gluten-free, if a concern)
- 3 tablespoons Regular, low-fat, or fat-free mayonnaise (gluten-free, if a concern)
- 3 Lettuce leaves, preferably romaine or iceberg
- 6 ¼-inch-thick tomato slices

Directions:

1. Preheat the air fryer to 375°F .

2. Wrap each chicken breast with 2 strips of bacon, spiraling the bacon around the meat, slightly overlapping the strips on each revolution. Start the second strip of bacon farther down the breast but on a line with the start of the first strip so they both end at a lined-up point on the chicken breast.

3. When the machine is at temperature, set the wrapped breasts bacon-seam side down in the basket with space between them. Air-fry undisturbed for 12 minutes, until the bacon is browned, crisp, and cooked through and an instant-read meat thermometer inserted into the center of a breast registers 165°F. You may need to add 2 minutes in the air fryer if the temperature is at 360°F.

4. Use kitchen tongs to transfer the breasts to a wire rack. Split the rolls open lengthwise and set them cut side down in the basket. Air-fry for 1 minute, or until warmed through.

5. Use kitchen tongs to transfer the rolls to a cutting board. Spread 1 tablespoon mayonnaise on the cut side of one half of each roll. Top with a chicken breast, lettuce leaf, and tomato slice. Serve warm.

Mexican Cheeseburgers

Servings: 4

Cooking Time: 22 Minutes

Ingredients:

- 1¼ pounds ground beef
- ¼ cup finely chopped onion
- ½ cup crushed yellow corn tortilla chips
- 1 (1.25-ounce) packet taco seasoning
- ¼ cup canned diced green chilies
- 1 egg, lightly beaten
- 4 ounces pepper jack cheese, grated
- 4 (12-inch) flour tortillas
- shredded lettuce, sour cream, guacamole, salsa (for topping)

Directions:

1. Combine the ground beef, minced onion, crushed tortilla chips, taco seasoning, green chilies, and egg in a large bowl. Mix thoroughly until combined – your hands are good tools for this. Divide the meat into four equal portions and shape each portion into an oval-shaped burger.

2. Preheat the air fryer to 370°F.

3. Air-fry the burgers for 18 minutes, turning them over halfway through the cooking time. Divide the cheese between the burgers, lower fryer to 340°F and air-fry for an additional 4 minutes to melt the cheese. (This will give you a burger that is medium-well. If you prefer your cheeseburger medium-rare, shorten the cooking time to about 15 minutes and then add the cheese and proceed with the recipe.)

4. While the burgers are cooking, warm the tortillas wrapped in aluminum foil in a 350°F oven, or in a skillet with a little oil over medium-high heat for a couple of minutes. Keep the tortillas warm until the burgers are ready.

5. To assemble the burgers, spread sour cream over three quarters of the tortillas and top each with some shredded lettuce and salsa. Place the Mexican cheeseburgers on the lettuce and top with guacamole. Fold the tortillas around the burger, starting with the bottom and then folding the sides in over the top. (A little sour cream can help hold the seam of the tortilla together.) Serve immediately.

Sausage And Pepper Heros

Servings: 3

Cooking Time: 11 Minutes

Ingredients:

- ➢ 3 links (about 9 ounces total) Sweet Italian sausages (gluten-free, if a concern)
- ➢ 1½ Medium red or green bell pepper(s), stemmed, cored, and cut into ½-inch-wide strips
- ➢ 1 medium Yellow or white onion(s), peeled, halved, and sliced into thin half-moons
- ➢ 3 Long soft rolls, such as hero, hoagie, or Italian sub rolls (gluten-free, if a concern), split open lengthwise
- ➢ For garnishing Balsamic vinegar
- ➢ For garnishing Fresh basil leaves

Directions:

1. Preheat the air fryer to 400°F.

2. When the machine is at temperature, set the sausage links in the basket in one layer and air-fry undisturbed for 5 minutes.

3. Add the pepper strips and onions. Continue air-frying, tossing and rearranging everything about once every minute, for 5 minutes, or until the sausages are browned and an instant-read meat thermometer inserted into one of the links registers 160°F.

4. Use a nonstick-safe spatula and kitchen tongs to transfer the sausages and vegetables to a cutting board. Set the rolls cut side down in the basket in one layer (working in batches as necessary) and air-fry undisturbed for 1 minute, to toast the rolls a bit and warm them up. Set 1 sausage with some pepper strips and onions in each warm roll, sprinkle balsamic vinegar over the sandwich fillings, and garnish with basil leaves.

White Bean Veggie Burgers

Servings: 3

Cooking Time: 13 Minutes

Ingredients:

- 1⅓ cups Drained and rinsed canned white beans
- 3 tablespoons Rolled oats (not quick-cooking or steel-cut; gluten-free, if a concern)
- 3 tablespoons Chopped walnuts
- 2 teaspoons Olive oil
- 2 teaspoons Lemon juice
- 1½ teaspoons Dijon mustard (gluten-free, if a concern)
- ¾ teaspoon Dried sage leaves
- ¼ teaspoon Table salt
- Olive oil spray
- 3 Whole-wheat buns or gluten-free whole-grain buns (if a concern), split open

Directions:

1. Preheat the air fryer to 400°F.

2. Place the beans, oats, walnuts, oil, lemon juice, mustard, sage, and salt in a food processor. Cover and process to make a coarse paste that will hold its shape, about like wet sugar-cookie dough, stopping the machine to scrape down the inside of the canister at least once.

3. Scrape down and remove the blade. With clean and wet hands, form the bean paste into two 4-inch patties for the small batch, three 4-inch patties for the medium, or four 4-inch patties for the large batch. Generously coat the patties on both sides with olive oil spray.

4. Set them in the basket with some space between them and air-fry undisturbed for 12 minutes, or until lightly brown and crisp at the edges. The tops of the burgers will feel firm to the touch.

5. Use a nonstick-safe spatula, and perhaps a flatware fork for balance, to transfer the burgers to a cutting board. Set the buns cut side down in the basket in one layer (working in batches as necessary) and air-fry undisturbed for 1 minute, to toast a bit and warm up. Serve the burgers warm in the buns.

Chili Cheese Dogs

Servings: 3

Cooking Time: 12 Minutes

Ingredients:

- ¾ pound Lean ground beef
- 1½ tablespoons Chile powder
- 1 cup plus 2 tablespoons Jarred sofrito
- 3 Hot dogs (gluten-free, if a concern)
- 3 Hot dog buns (gluten-free, if a concern), split open lengthwise
- 3 tablespoons Finely chopped scallion
- 9 tablespoons (a little more than 2 ounces) Shredded Cheddar cheese

Directions:

1. Crumble the ground beef into a medium or large saucepan set over medium heat. Brown well, stirring often to break up the clumps. Add the chile powder and cook for 30 seconds, stirring the whole time. Stir in the sofrito and bring to a simmer. Reduce the heat to low and simmer, stirring occasionally, for 5 minutes. Keep warm.

2. Preheat the air fryer to 400°F.

3. When the machine is at temperature, put the hot dogs in the basket and air-fry undisturbed for 10 minutes, or until the hot dogs are bubbling and blistered, even a little crisp.

4. Use kitchen tongs to put the hot dogs in the buns. Top each with a ½ cup of the ground beef mixture, 1 tablespoon of the minced scallion, and 3 tablespoons of the cheese. (The scallion should go under the cheese so it superheats and wilts a bit.) Set the filled hot dog buns in the basket and air-fry undisturbed for 2 minutes, or until the cheese has melted.

5. Remove the basket from the machine. Cool the chili cheese dogs in the basket for 5 minutes before serving.

Chicken Apple Brie Melt

Servings: 3

Cooking Time: 13 Minutes

Ingredients:

- 3 5- to 6-ounce boneless skinless chicken breasts
- Vegetable oil spray
- 1½ teaspoons Dried herbes de Provence
- 3 ounces Brie, rind removed, thinly sliced
- 6 Thin cored apple slices
- 3 French rolls (gluten-free, if a concern)
- 2 tablespoons Dijon mustard (gluten-free, if a concern)

Directions:

1. Preheat the air fryer to 375°F .

2. Lightly coat all sides of the chicken breasts with vegetable oil spray. Sprinkle the breasts evenly with the herbes de Provence.

3. When the machine is at temperature, set the breasts in the basket and air-fry undisturbed for 10 minutes.

4. Top the chicken breasts with the apple slices, then the cheese. Air-fry undisturbed for 2 minutes, or until the cheese is melty and bubbling.

5. Use a nonstick-safe spatula and kitchen tongs, for balance, to transfer the breasts to a cutting board. Set the rolls in the basket and air-fry for 1 minute to warm through. (Putting them in the machine without splitting them keeps the insides very soft while the outside gets a little crunchy.)

6. Transfer the rolls to the cutting board. Split them open lengthwise, then spread 1 teaspoon mustard on each cut side. Set a prepared chicken breast on the bottom of a roll and close with its top, repeating as necessary to make additional sandwiches. Serve warm.

Thanksgiving Turkey Sandwiches

Servings: 3

Cooking Time: 10 Minutes

Ingredients:

- 1½ cups Herb-seasoned stuffing mix (not cornbread-style; gluten-free, if a concern)
- 1 Large egg white(s)
- 2 tablespoons Water
- 3 5- to 6-ounce turkey breast cutlets
- Vegetable oil spray
- 4½ tablespoons Purchased cranberry sauce, preferably whole berry
- ⅛ teaspoon Ground cinnamon
- ⅛ teaspoon Ground dried ginger
- 4½ tablespoons Regular, low-fat, or fat-free mayonnaise (gluten-free, if a concern)
- 6 tablespoons Shredded Brussels sprouts
- 3 Kaiser rolls (gluten-free, if a concern), split open

Directions:

1. Preheat the air fryer to 375°F .

2. Put the stuffing mix in a heavy zip-closed bag, seal it, lay it flat on your counter, and roll a rolling pin over the bag to crush the stuffing mix to the consistency of rough sand. (Or you can pulse the stuffing mix to the desired consistency in a food processor.)

3. Set up and fill two shallow soup plates or small pie plates on your counter: one for the egg white(s), whisked with the water until foamy; and one for the ground stuffing mix.

4. Dip a cutlet in the egg white mixture, coating both sides and letting any excess egg white slip back into the rest. Set the cutlet in the ground stuffing mix and coat it evenly on both sides, pressing gently to coat well on both sides. Lightly coat the cutlet on both sides with vegetable oil spray, set it aside, and continue dipping and coating the remaining cutlets in the same way.

5. Set the cutlets in the basket and air-fry undisturbed for 10 minutes, or until crisp and brown. Use kitchen tongs to transfer the cutlets to a wire rack to cool for a few minutes.

6. Meanwhile, stir the cranberry sauce with the cinnamon and ginger in a small bowl. Mix the shredded Brussels sprouts and mayonnaise in a second bowl until the vegetable is evenly coated.

7. Build the sandwiches by spreading about 1½ tablespoons of the cranberry mixture on the cut side of the bottom half of each roll. Set a cutlet on top, then spread about 3 tablespoons of the Brussels sprouts mixture evenly over the cutlet. Set the other half of the roll on top and serve warm.

9 781803 200125

Printed by Libri Plureos GmbH in Hamburg, Germany